If you stand by my teaching,
you are truly my disciples; you will
know the truth, and the truth will set you free.
JOHN 8:31-32

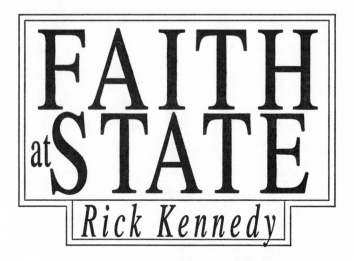

FAITH at STATE

Rick Kennedy

A Handbook
for Christians
at Secular
Universities

InterVarsity Press
Downers Grove, Illinois

InterVarsity Press® is the book-publishing division of InterVarsity Christian Fellowship®, a student movement active on campus at hundreds of universities, colleges and schools of nursing in the United States of America, and a member movement of the International Fellowship of Evangelical Students. For information about local and regional activities, write Public Relations Dept., InterVarsity Christian Fellowship, 6400 Schroeder Rd., P.O. Box 7895, Madison, WI 53707-7895.

All quotations from the Bible are from The Revised English Bible (Oxford University Press and Cambridge University Press, 1989).

Cover photograph: Bob Krist

ISBN 0-8308-1622-4

Printed in the United States of America ♻

Library of Congress Cataloging-in-Publication Data

Kennedy, Rick, 1958-
    Faith at state: a handbook for Christians at secular universities
/Rick Kennedy.
     p.   cm.
    Includes bibliographical references.
    ISBN 0-8303-1622-4 (alk. paper)
    1. College students—United States—Religious life. 2. College
students—United States—Conduct of life. 3. Public universities
and colleges—United States—Religion. 4. Witness bearing
(Christianity) I. Title.
BV4531.2.K455   1995
248.8'34—dc20   *95-30877*
                                                                 CIP

20	19	18	17	16	15	14	13	12	11	10	9	8	7	6	5	4	3	2	1
12	11	10	09	08	07	06	05	04	03	02	01	00	99	98	97	96	95		

Dedicated to my grandparents, parents and brothers:
Arthur and Helen Barber, G. Robert and Donna, Kirk and Mark;

First Presbyterian Church, Salinas, California (1972-1976),
especially Bruce Rowlinson, Tom Elson and Steve Yamaguchi;

the Sequoia dorm fellowship (1976-1978),
California Polytechnic State University at San Luis Obispo;

the Four Square Gospel Church of San Luis Obispo
and its boarding house on Los Osos Street (1976-1978),
especially Ray Vineyard;

the Nazarene churches in San Luis Obispo and Santa Barbara
(1976-1981), especially Ken Meredith;

Redwood Camp, Mt. Hermon Christian Conference Center
(1977-1978), especially Cynthia Peterson and Susan Barbaria,
the latter of whom married me;

the folks who hung out at the apartment
on El Nido Street, Isla Vista (1978-1979),
especially David Hale, Pat Dollard and Mark Claddis;

Married Student Housing morning talks
with Chuck Ahern and Miles Woodleif (1980-1983);

Dos Pueblos High School Young Life (1980-1983),
especially Matt Bell, Jeff Cann, Kathy Bride,
Kelly Soifer, Vance, Isau, Bob, Ray, Alex, Roger, Bob,
and all the rest in that wild and intense time;

St. Michael's University Episcopal Church (1982-1987),
especially Gary Commins, George Hall and Tim Vivian;

the history department,
University of California, Santa Barbara (1978-1987),
especially Harold Kirker, Jeff Russell, Cameron Airhart,
Miriam Raub, Barry Ryan, Cheryl Riggs, Abraham Friesen
and Jon Rainbow, and the members of our ad hoc
lunch group, Faith and the Intellectual Life;

all of which and whom taught me
about being a Christian at a secular university.

Acknowledgments

Many conversations with students lie behind the statements and assumptions in this book. I can't thank enough the students who have taken the time to visit my office in order to discuss ideas, perspectives and facts. Several academic colleagues read the first draft of this book and offered their own perspectives: Tim Vivian, Jeff Russell, John Newman, John James and James Barry. Three students read a draft: Jon Faith, Tim Wood and Cory Blatz. Two ministers offered extensive comments: Tom Elson and Mark Gardner. Cindy Peterson, Kelly Soifer, Donna Kennedy, Kirk Kennedy, Dick Dosker, Miriam Raub, Vivian and Barry Ryan also offered advice and encouragement. Rodney Clapp of InterVarsity Press offered editorial help.

This book was mostly written from Thanksgiving through January of 1993-1994, a time of severe snowstorms, vacations and canceled classes. I wanted to write something useful in the tradition of Augustine's *Enchiridion* and Cotton Mather's *Manuductio,* handbooks that bring together what is already known while sparking new action, new inquiry, new confidence and new faith.

Preface

I understand the fear that many contemporary Christians have of the secular university. I went to one and now teach in one. I am sure my parents still pray that I will not be too influenced by my surroundings. My older brother became a philosophy major at a big state university and for a few years gave up on Christianity. When my younger brother was choosing a college, my mother asked me if she should encourage him to go to a small Christian college so that there would be less chance of his following in my older brother's footsteps. He eventually went to the same state university at which his older brothers started. It was so inexpensive in comparison! It was also where other friends went.

I think much of the best undergraduate education going on in America is happening at small Christian colleges, but this is not a book about them. Most Christians go to big public universities.

I meet Christian students every semester in my classes, and many of them act as if they have been coached by their mothers to be wary of what we professors profess. Students *should* be wary. All of us professors too easily confuse academic knowledge with wisdom and truth. But if a Christian is attending a public university, he or she should be coached in more than just fear. The Christian student should be taught how to get the most out of the university experience so that he or she can better serve God.

I love the modern university. I have spent most of my life in public education and all of my years in college at big state schools. There my Christianity was challenged and strengthened. Through the prayers of my parents, daily Bible reading, discussions with fellow students and professors, and the support of local churches, I thrived in modern public education. American public education is my intellectual mother, my alma mater. When I hear it criticized and judged to be some evil force in society, I want to respond with a more balanced judgment.

This book is not a defense of public universities; rather, it simply recognizes that public universities have to reflect the values of the society of taxpayers who support them. To the extent that our society has diverse values and taxpayers adhere to multiple religions, public universities have to reflect the variety.

But just as there is a role for serious Christians in society, even though we are a minority, there is also a role for us in public universities. This is a book about Christian learning within public and secular universities.

Knowing Our Place on Campus

Christians can thrive at the university, in debates, in studying, in listening. Big secular universities are filled with the foolish and the wise, the good and the evil, the seductive and the holy. Christians must discern the one from the other. They must stand firmly for the *rationality* of being a Christian, in the full meaning of the word.

We Christians too often have given up our rightful place at universities. Universities are important places and Christians cannot afford to be silent on campus. What is at stake when Christians are silent or weak in universities?

At the heart of all the problems facing Western civilization—the general nervousness and restlessness, the dearth of grace and beauty and quality and peace of soul, the manifold blemishes and perversions of personal character; problems of the family and of social relations in general, problems of economics and politics, problems of the media, problems affecting the school itself and the church itself, problems of the international order—at the heart of the crisis in Western civilization lies the state of mind and the spirit of universities.

Are we to be silent or weak when so much is at stake? Universities, for sure, cause problems just as often as they solve problems, but problem solving is the goal. Universities are filled with good intentions. Jump in and roll up your sleeves. The work is good and the goals great. Whatever is good is of God.

Most professors think of themselves as practical people at work solving the world's problems and increasing the world's knowledge. Most professors feel a calling, even when they are not sure who is calling. They are practical people hoping to do good.

Many non-Christian university professors think that Christians are speculative, impractical idealists living far removed from the needs of the real world. Christians, they think, live with their heads in the clouds. You and I know that's not true. Christians both feel a calling and know the caller. We have a deep concern for the creation because we know the Creator. We have the big picture of eternity and the knowledge that humans have the dignity and equality of eternal souls. Christianity is practical—and not only practical but true!

Christians need to serve side by side with the practical people of universities who are at work solving problems. We have a responsibility to be involved at every level in public universities, where public funds are spent for the purpose of making a better, more informed world. Don't shirk the responsibility. Don't blow the opportunity.

You Know More Than You Think You Know

"You know more than you think you know." That was what the preface of Dr. Spock's handbook told my mother when she was trying to handle her sons' cuts, bruises and fevers in the 1950s and 1960s. It's a comforting truth in medicine, and even more of a truth in the modern university, where part of the educational process is designed to break down your confidences and build new ones. I hope this book strengthens your confidence in what you have already experienced from God, so that you can withstand any attempts by both well-meaning and deliberately misleading professors to shake your faith in Christ.

As a Christian you know more than you think you know. You know that God is active and that creation is not ruled by impersonal "forces." You know creation has a purpose, that order rules over apparent chaos. You know that love, courage, sacrifice and joy are not mere genetics and chemical reactions. You know that families are not merely human institutions designed for economic purposes. You know that truth exists, even if you only have the barest glimmer of what it might be. You know Jesus and have experienced the Holy Spirit. You have felt the power of spiritual reality and can't be convinced that it was merely a chemical imbalance in your mind. You know that humans are not machines but that we have eternal souls. You know that God loves you and all of us for no good reason. You look at a flower, feel the wind on a spring day or watch kids playing soccer, and you know that a benevolent God exists. You are sometimes overwhelmed with joy or love, and you realize you are experiencing an inkling of something much greater.

But you still have things to learn. This is not only a book to inspire your confidence in what you already know and to protect your Christianity from some of what you learn in classes. God is the Creator of knowledge and rationality. As a Christian you are obligated to embrace truth wherever it is found and to learn the best methods human beings have developed to discover new knowledge. If we learn new things, true things, we are obligated to incorporate them into our lives and our understanding of God. If we learn that some of the things we previously thought are false, then we are obligated to abandon the wrong.

More than anything else, I hope that this handbook will show you that rationality is a wild and wonderful gift of God that cannot be boxed in by anybody, fenced in by any institution or limited in any way by mere humanity. Universities, at their best, are places where such boxes, fences and limits are broken open or torn down.

As a child of God made in the divine image, you live entwined in that wild and wonderful partnership between God's mind and your own. The modern university has an important and special role in our society: helping us to use our minds better. We must love universities for what they are, not fear them for what they can do to us or what some of their professors or students say about God.

The motto of the university I graduated from is "Let there be light," and the motto of the university I teach at is "Light and Truth." Any place where light and truth are important values should be a place where Christians are at home, since Jesus said he was both the truth and the light. Be wary of the university, but also love the university.

What follows is St. Bonaventure's preface to his handbook on being a rational Christian. There is no more concise or better advice to university Christians than this:

> First, therefore, I invite the reader
> to the groans of prayer
> through Christ crucified,
> through whose blood
> we are cleansed from the filth of vice—
> so that he not believe
> that reading is sufficient without unction,
> speculation without devotion,
> investigation without wonder,
> observation without joy,
> work without piety,
> knowledge without love,
> understanding without humility,
> endeavor without divine grace,
> reflection as a mirror without divinely inspired wisdom.
> To those, therefore, predisposed by divine grace,
> the humble and the pious,
> the contrite and the devout,
> those anointed with the oil of gladness,
> the lovers of divine wisdom, and
> those inflamed with desire for it,

to those wishing to give themselves
to glorifying, wondering at and even savoring God,
I propose the following considerations,
suggesting that the mirror presented by the external world
is of little or no value
unless the mirror of our mind
has been cleaned and polished.
(*The Mind's Journey into God,* translated by Ewart Cousins)

Part I

University Life & Values

– 1 –

The Village

Thomas Jefferson, the principal founder and designer of the University of Virginia, called his university an "Academical Village." It's a nice image. Universities and colleges are villages, most set in parklike surroundings but some in urban squalor. They have police forces, road-maintenance crews and garbage collectors. Small businesses thrive: bookstores, hot-dog stands and recreation shops. Usually there is a newspaper, often a radio station. An administration runs the village, but they usually call it "the physical plant." An administrator once defined a university as various academic departments united by a central heating system. I prefer "village" because universities are communities of people and bureaucracies that are rarely rushed. Almost everyone has time to chat, gossip or take a walk.

Clark Kerr, president of the University of California system in the 1960s, called the modern university a "multiversity" and compared academic institutions to cities rather than villages. I disagree. Even at big universities—for example, Ohio State and the Universities of Minnesota, Michigan and California at Los Angeles—life is more villagelike than citylike. They are big schools of forty to sixty thousand students; however, the pace of life is still slow in comparison to that of an urban professional. Walk across campus and you are bound to wave at a few friends or see several classmates. A former professor or two will be recognized. The professor may not remember your name, but a friendly nod of the head is the standard form of polite recognition. The gardeners and janitors, many of them busier than anyone else on campus, will become familiar figures.

The academic village is not an anonymous city; rather, it is a pleasantly active place full of face-to-face recognition and lots of organizations that welcome new members. Students should get involved and think of the village as their own. Attending classes, choosing a major and trying to discover their vocation are their most important roles on campus; however, they should also join in village life. Many students work part time for the university on the gardening, painting and cafeteria crews. Others work as assistants to secretaries or as salespeople in the bookstore. One benefit of such jobs is that they have the opportunity to meet the less glamorous village members, members who are often overlooked, since most of the focus of the university is on professors and students. Campus clubs and sporting events are also important to village life and offer many ways for new students to become members of the community.

Jesus said that the first and greatest commandment is to love God and the second greatest commandment is to love your neighbor as yourself, not to do your homework or memorize conjugations of some verb. The villagelike setting of the university is a wonderful place to practice loving neighbors. Become a member. Join the newspaper staff or student government. Rise up to become arts editor or vice president. Learn to serve. Learn to love others while working side by side. The world outside a university, whether in newspapers, government or almost any other job, is a lot harsher than the one in the academic village. Practice love in the one and build on it in the other.

In the village you also have great opportunities to practice being a Christian. The modern university is full of all types of people and organizations, much like the larger world it prepares students for. Practicing Christians are a minority in the world and a minority at universities, but just as the world has not been abandoned by God, neither has the university. Most campuses have a variety of Christian organizations called "parachurch" because they are Christian clubs rather than real churches. I will talk more about them a little later. Churches are more important. They are the body of Christ in a way that no Christian fellowship organization can be. Many campuses have churches connected to them, usually funded as missionary ventures by large denominations.

Join a Church

I belonged to several different community churches in different denominations during my early years as a student; however, I had my best church experience after joining an Episcopal campus church with a small building and a young vicar/chaplain. Students and elderly people from a nearby retirement center dominated the congregation of about seventy people. As students we sat on the governing board that advised the vicar; we ran the stewardship campaigns; we voted on the budget, deciding the priorities for outreach, building maintenance and worship supplies. We *were* the church in a way that I had never experienced in larger churches, where college students were usually not considered full adults. I learned much about Christian responsibility and true membership in the body of Christ.

Through my church I also had an important Christian role in the non-Christian academic village to which I belonged. Universities are not godless. Some of the classes, activities and people may be godless; however, Christians, their churches and Christianity are alive and active too. Churches are usually part of every campus village. Across the street from my Episcopal church was a larger church run by the Roman Catholic Paulist fathers. A Methodist and an evangelical church were a few blocks the other way. Also nearby was the University Religious Conference (URC), which offered an umbrella organization and building for campus ministers, including a Jewish organization.

A Christian should not feel alone at college any more than he or she should feel alone in any American community. Seek out the Christian churches. Where the churches are, there are the varieties of folk who make up the body of Christ. Where the churches are, there are the grassroots of Christian activity on a university campus. An active campus church will have connections with Christian professors and advisory roles to the administration and will be active in everything from ministering in times of campus disaster to supporting political/religious demonstrations. Join a church. There is no foundation stronger for a Christian at the university or in life.

Commuter Students

Maybe you have read so far thinking that I am talking only about "traditional" college students: eighteen to twenty-five years old, unmarried, living in a campus dormitory or in a student-dominated apartment building. I'm not. Most college students in America do not live on campus. They live with parents or spouse and/or kids and go to commuter-oriented public colleges. Most college students in America have jobs helping them to pay their tuition; therefore, they spend only a few hours a day on campus. No matter what your situation, if you are a student you are a member of the university. Your job is to be as active a member as you can.

I teach history at a commuter-oriented regional state university. Our goal is to be the university to citizens of Indiana living in the Louisville, Kentucky, metropolitan area. We have admission requirements but will waive them for anyone who can breathe and keep a positive checkbook balance. After a couple of semesters, if a student can't get up to university speed, he or she is eased out. Although the most active students on campus tend to be young and unmarried, my classes usually have several thirty- or forty-something women with children at home, and perhaps someone who recently left military service. The older students are often heroes trying to make their families' lives better. Many can't get all of every assignment read. Many have to cut my class when their children are sick. Often we have to do some professor-student negotiating to help them fit family, work and school together.

Do they have time for student government or writing for the student newspaper? Probably not, although some are the best student leaders we have. Do they have time to join a campus Christian group? Probably not, but I certainly hope that they are involved in a local church.

Every student, however, should be involved as much as possible both in their studies and in the university community. No one should slide anonymously through the curriculum thinking it is merely a means to an end. Parents commuting to school in order to make a career change or get better job opportunities are as welcome in the university as singles living in dormitories. Every student must do what he or she can to both get the most out of and give the most to the university. Students of whatever stage in life should embrace the university community to the extent to which they are able.

Love your school. Love your opportunity. If you begin to feel your classes are just a series of hoops for you to jump through, hoops that are unduly complicating your life, then you need to stop and pray for wisdom—wisdom to set priorities and decide whether to stay or to leave the university.

Love Your School

Embrace the type of academic village you are part of. Don't yearn for some "better" school or think that your education is something "less" than someone else's. Most students in America attend regional state universities associated with a large mother campus. Students who go to compass-point colleges—places with names that include designations such as "southern," or worse, "southeast," or worse yet, "southeast central"—usually feel that the mother campuses without compass-point names are better. I know students at Big Ten mother campuses who think their school isn't as good as big universities on the coasts. I know students at big coastal universities frustrated that they didn't get into the Ivy League or Stanford. I have eaten lunch in Harvard Yard with a group of graduate students and listened to them complain about their program at Harvard.

Society forces students to rank schools as better or worse. Don't give in. Most Americans go to colleges with no special prestige or reputation. They pick universities that are inexpensive, close and able to serve their needs. If a school fits your complex needs, then it is the best school for you. Embrace it. Be true to it.

I recently read *The University: An Owner's Manual* by the former dean of arts and sciences at Harvard University, Henry Rosovsky. It's a delightful book if the reader wants to understand life at what the author calls "the best" and "most selective" universities—by which he means Harvard, Yale, UC Berkeley, Michigan, Stanford and maybe a few other schools. Such universities have movies and novels made about them, their administrators become ambassadors or baseball commissioners, and their professors are interviewed by the national media. But most of the educational work in America is not happening at those universities. To be sure there are benefits to being a student or professor at Harvard or UC Berkeley; however, those benefits do not always outweigh the benefits of *not* being at Harvard or Berkeley. The worst problem with such schools is they don't encourage humility. Pride is a deadly sin that can kill people's ability to learn from each other.

I insist that the best education in America is available at every university in every class—Big Ten campus or regional commuter campus, big library or small, professor with worldwide or merely local reputation, professor only half sober at ten o'clock in the morning or bright and inspiring at all times. The best education is available, but only a small number of students embrace their opportunity for education. The best education is what you make out of the resources available—teachers, books, experiences and community. Education is what happens inside a student's mind and is effected by an act of the will, by desire. As a professor I can assign work, help interpret and organize, explain and pass on information; however, the best students always outpace me and the class. The best students are thinking with open minds. They ask questions I can't answer. They go to the library. They order books through interlibrary loan. They test their ideas with their friends. They listen. They keep thinking. They compare what they learn with their experience. They delve deeply into their own experience and knowledge while at the same time reaching out to embrace new knowledge. That is America's best education and it is happening among some members of every university, whether twenty-two-year-old singles or forty-four-year-old mothers, whether at com-pass-point colleges or at Harvard.

But more on that later. At present I am simply beginning with a view of the university as a village. As in any American village, there are good and bad people, churches and bars, sad cases of destroyed lives and glorious cases of fulfilled promise. Ideally everyone in the village is there to serve each other and the university's high purpose. From the gardeners to the professors, with a dominant role allotted to the students, all share citizenship in the village.

For Christians, the village laws are simple. There are only two: first love the God of truth with all your heart, mind and strength, and then love your neighbor as yourself.

−2−

The Knowledge Industry
Majors, General Education Requirements, Grades & the GPA

C lark Kerr, the university administrator who called the village a "multiversity," also coined the term *knowledge industry* to describe the character of the modern university. The true university, for which this book serves as a handbook, is the dynamic spirit, intellectual methods and community that have characterized higher education from the ancient Hebrews and Greeks to today. However, in our society the true university is fused to a knowledge industry designed as an integral part of a national and international economy in which companies and governments compete for the services of students and professors. Grades, majors, GPA ratings and general education requirements are aspects of the knowledge industry with which this handbook is not much concerned. I will devote just a little time to those things here in order to get them out of the way.

Grades, majors and especially the GPA are very modern additions to educational institutions. They became widespread in the early twentieth century after big business and big government began funding universities. They are an aspect of a measurement mentality in business and government. John D. Rockefeller, the rich oil baron, built the University of Chicago about a hundred years ago. Over one of the doors is carved in stone: "When you cannot measure . . . your knowledge is . . . meager . . . and unsatisfactory." In big business as in big education, productivity emphasizes measurement and standardization. A product should have a measurement attached to it that rates its quality. A product, for example a window or carburetor, should be standardized, so that a replacement window or carburetor can be easily acquired and installed when the first breaks down. The measurement mentality helped make American business great, and it also helped build American university systems.

Beginning a little over one hundred years ago, business leaders, along with politicians, began believing that strong universities would make for a strong America. They joined together to support and guide an educational boom. New universities were built across the country. And just as American business was experimenting with all sorts of methods to mass-produce products and services, a powerful class of university presidents and educational reformers began experimenting with methods of mass production, standardization and quality control in education.

The knowledge industry begun at that time makes a student into the product of an assembly line. The university policies that most affect a student's day-to-day university existence—grades, majors, general education requirements and degree requirements—were developed out of the mentality that also designed the automobile assembly line. The Founding Fathers of the United States were mostly college educated, but they never took a graded test in college. They did not have majors. They certainly had no GPAs. Mostly their performance was explained to them by their teachers. If they needed to prove to a future employer that they had performed well in college, the employer could talk with or write a letter to the prospective employee's former teacher.

When education is mass-produced, however, such a system is outdated. Several universities designed in the 1960s tried to go back to a preindustrial system. Most of them had to give it up, largely because employers and graduate schools wanted a GPA rating and not a written or spoken evaluation. St. John's College in Annapolis and Santa Fe continues to avoid grades, majors and the GPA, but it survives by being very small and selective.

Modern mass education is an assembly line. As on an assembly line, a student's quality as an end product has to be stamped with a specialty (the major) and rated with a number (the GPA). As in any industry, "efficiency" has to be imposed and "success" has to be measured. In the early twentieth century, frequent testing was instituted; grades of ABCDF were developed, majors created and registrar offices expanded to store and disseminate quality-control information. One university professor wrote in 1918 that American universities had adopted more than just the industrial model—they had taken on many qualities of American prisons!

As you can tell, I do not appreciate the industrial aspects of mass education, especially at the university level. The bigness of universities, along with their direct ties to local, state and national politics, forces them to spend more time than smaller private colleges on standardization and systems to rate quality. American public education, however, is cheaper and gives more opportunity to more people than any other structure of higher education in the world. As with most things in life, we must take the good with the bad.

The Example of Indiana University

My employer can serve as an example of the type of things that happened across the country when the knowledge industry was developing. Indiana University began during the college-building boom of the 1820s. At that time state governments and churches were working together to found what would become great universities. This alliance of church and state was built on the hope of spreading education, since both churches and governments need members and citizens who can think clearly, vote rationally and understand that right thinking should lead to right living. From the start, Indiana University's leaders followed national educational trends. One trend was to diminish the alliance of church and state in universities while encouraging an alliance of big business and big government. In the 1880s IU adopted the "elective system," which gave students freedom to pick among a variety of classes taught by professors with narrow specialties. Although the elective system diversified education at IU, it was counterproductive to the rising mentality of the knowledge industry. The development of majors, general education requirements, grades and the GPA at IU began as attempts to hedge in the chaos of the elective system of classes. This elective system allowed the "product" too much control in designing its own production. The knowledge industry needed to design systems of majors and general education requirements to hedge in that independence.

The choice of a major requires the student to specialize in one field. The major is usually designed to train undergraduates so that they can move easily into graduate studies in the same field. The major represents a specialized career track. The goal of general education requirements is also to set boundaries on a student's freedom to choose any class in the elective system. But while the aim of the major system is specialized expertise, that of the general education requirements is broad cultural knowledge of diverse methods of scientific investigation and artistic aesthetics. IU first followed national trends by instituting the necessity of choosing a major and organizing faculty by departments. IU then later joined in the never-ending process of regulating general education requirements.

To facilitate standardization and quality control among many universities, accreditation organizations formed, which IU joined. For accreditation to work, the various universities had to adopt, voluntarily, the same systems of quality control. The end result, as with the automobile industry, is the amazing level of structural sameness between universities in America. IU became one of the many state universities whose system of majors and general education reforms was guided by the regulatory trends of a knowledge industry increasingly dominated by accreditation systems.

Accreditation organizations also encouraged the creation of grades and the GPA. In 1908 the IU faculty recommended the use of grades A, B, C and D, with anything worse being defined by the course instructor as "conditioned" or "failed." The letters were correlated to a four-point scale and also to percentages. During this period Ernest H. Lindley was the head of a campus committee pushing for the use of tests and measurements to ensure quality control. Lindley was a "professional psychologist and educationist" and typical of the type of theorists who want modern education to follow the model of industrial standardization and quantification. His committee surveyed four other universities and found that IU gave a higher percentage of A's and B's than the others. IU, he insisted, must bring the percentage of its grades into line with other universities. Also in 1909, IU had been invited to join the Association of American Universities, which set national standards of quality control. To keep its membership and to respond to Lindley's committee, the faculty passed resolutions in 1910 for instructors to be policed so as not to give too many high grades and for students to be more tightly policed during testing.

By the 1940s, the knowledge industry as it affects students was largely in place at IU and throughout America generally. Majors, general education requirements, grades and the GPA had all been instituted, in order to standardize and measure the quality of the product. In the 1950s and 1960s another educational boom swept the country, and new universities were built in almost every corner of every state. Big government, especially Cold War politics combined with New Deal idealism, dominated the mentality of this boom. A democratic urge demanded that universities reach out to the people. The university should go to the people rather than make the people come to the university. Democracy requires an educated citizenry, and so the universities took on a missionary mentality to bring education to everyone. America is much better for it.

IU expanded in the 1960s and 1970s from one campus to eight. The University of California in the 1950s and 1960s expanded from two campuses to nine. The university I graduated from and the university I teach at did not exist as degree-granting universities when I was born. My generation was raised in a chaotic atmosphere of educational expansion. Today's college student is being educated in a period of attempts to organize and stabilize universities after the boom. Indiana University Southeast, the 1970s campus of IU at which I teach, spends lots of energy trying to figure out how best to serve students and community while still following a university model created for a knowledge industry. This is an exciting time of transformation for modern universities, and students have the opportunity to participate on committees and in student government. If you have the energy and time, join in.

Since the 1940s, American universities have been recognized worldwide as the most productive and democratic system of higher education in the world. The American public university, more than any other American institution, embodies our country's commitment to being a land of opportunity and a land of educated citizens who can vote intelligently. IU, especially the mother campus at Bloomington, became after the 1940s one of America's greatest universities. Walk the Bloomington campus and you are on the greatest jewel in the crown of Indiana's taxpayers. Architecturally it is beautiful. Educationally it gives an inexpensive opportunity to any student willing to study hard. It bolsters the economy of the state and supplies it with a large percentage of its best civil servants. Graduate students come from around the world to gain knowledge in the hills of southern Indiana that can transform their own countries. Indiana University is a wonderful institution. It is also a cog in the knowledge industry, controlled by outside forces of standardization and measurement.

The American university is more productive than any other university type in the world. The American knowledge industry succeeds. However, we must be careful when we say such things.

The Limits of the Knowledge Industry

The knowledge industry has been very successful in some areas but a failure in others. Modern critics of university education and research methods are right to not let the successes blind them to the big picture. Today, significant figures such as federal secretaries of education, many political and business leaders, and even more faculty and administrators have begun to publicly state that the knowledge industry has not necessarily produced better businesspeople, teachers, politicians, doctors, clergy, lawyers, artists, musicians, poets and philosophers. This is true. Later in the book I will discuss some of the tradeoffs university disciplines make when they are striving toward productivity.

Also, the problem both with the knowledge industry and with the critics of the knowledge industry is that they talk of students as "products." Inconsistently, students are sometimes also called "consumers." Students are never products and are not consumers. They are *members.* They are members of a university community that is dedicated to the goal of learning more in the hope of serving society better. The knowledge industry is dominant in the registrar's office and in the administration building, but it is not dominant in good classrooms—and the interaction of students and professors in classrooms is the core of the university.

The knowledge industry cannot produce a quality product. Students make themselves. Students are not cars. They are not products. They are active participants in creating themselves. God gave all of us that freedom. As much as politicians, administrators, accreditation organizations, professional associations and businesspeople would like to think that they control the quality of your education, they don't. You control your education.

Join with faculty as members of a self-help and community-help society. The true university is not an industry, not numbers and letters rating students, and certainly not a set of buildings. The true university is what happens among the members—including both faculty and students.

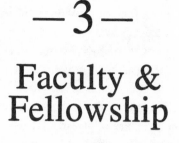

Faculty & Fellowship

There are lots of good faculty members at every school. The job of the student is to seek out the good ones and avoid the bad ones. But what makes a good teacher? The most important quality of a good teacher is commitment to students and the subject of the class. Knowledge of the subject is, of course, important. Some of the best courses, however, are small classes where the professor and the students embark together to learn about a subject. Research seminars often work this way.

Many of your best teachers will not be Christians, and you might even find that some of your Christian professors are not good teachers. Good teaching does not require conscious love of God. It requires a sense of calling—vocation. Many non-Christians have done great and wonderful things because of a vague sense that someone or something is calling them, even though they have no idea who or what.

Teaching is a high calling and a wonderful job. Throughout the Bible the vocation of teacher is accorded much respect and responsibility. Throughout the history of the United States our public policy has emphasized educating as many citizens as possible and allocating the necessary funds to educate teachers. Good teachers make for a good nation. Quintilian, one of the greatest teachers of Rome, wrote that teachers stand in the place of parents. He used the famous phrase *in loco parentis,* "in the place of parents," which has passed through history down to our own time as the motto for the responsibility and love that are supposed to invigorate the relationship between teachers and students.

Recently, however, the ideals of parental responsibility and love in the teaching profession have been radically realigned. Teachers at all levels of education, whether Christian or not, walk a tightrope. State legislators, administrators and taxpayers, whether politically liberal or conservative, want to use schools to reform the ills of society. Politics has politicized teaching, so that teachers are regularly attacked in the press for what they do or don't do. It should be noted that teachers' unions and lobbies have made the situation even worse because they seek to protect teachers' rights before they seek to promote good education.

Good teachers, as a result, have to cultivate the ability to not listen to their administrators, legislators and the winds of public sentiment. This causes many problems for teachers, but it must be done if students are to be treated as individual human beings rather than fodder for statistics and social engineering.

The Discerning Student

Education is mostly the student's responsibility. Approach every teacher and class as a new opportunity, even when you don't like the teacher or the material. Most of the times I have encountered students hating my classes or the classes of other professors it was because of classroom styles, not the material covered. In the classroom, style is nothing, subject everything.

If you are the kind of person who is *very* organized—that is, you make your bed every morning, your shoes are organized by color in your closet, and your car glove compartment has the maps alphabetically or geographically ordered—then you are most likely to appreciate teachers who are well organized and write neat outlines on overhead projectors. My shoes are thrown in a pile in my closet, and I tend to give lectures while marching back and forth and flinging my arms around, without following any notes. I have had students complain about my teaching because they can't take tidy notes. I have other students who like my class for its free and open, give-and-take style.

I suggest that students accept a professor's style. Style is not important.

The wise student needs to be a discerning listener. Professors in the classroom say many things that are not "the whole truth and nothing but the truth." Even in classes where there seems to be nothing but dry facts and memorization, the teachers are organizing the information to appeal to the students. In any performance situation the performer will shade things to keep the audience interested. Professors do the same.

For example, a friend of mine told me that in his economics class the professor said that marriage is an economic union and that people get married when it is more economically efficient than staying single. This is of course true and absurd at the same time. Marriage is *partly* an economic union, but surely the professor did not mean to simplify such a complex human decision as to whether to get married into the mere result of a calculator. The professor was probably making a bold statement to get the students' attention and to make them think in economic terms. It worked. The student remembered the statement a decade after graduating. In a situation such as this, the student has a responsibility to turn what the professor says to its best use.

A recent article about a certain bombastic professor in Maine was titled "Art Historian as Provocateur." This very popular teacher apparently casts all sorts of ideas into the classroom, hoping to catch the students' attention. "I'm not interested in saying the last word on anything," he says. "My goal is to open up discussion."

I have had professors like him. They can be very exciting, but you have to weed out what is brilliant from what is foolish. As a Christian, you may find their lack of concern for the truth disconcerting. Their statements have a promiscuous ring—it sounds as if they believe in discussion for discussion's sake. But if you find yourself in such a provocative classroom, don't rebel. Enjoy the freedom and learn. Turn the discussion to good use in your life.

Wide-open discussion can be enlightening. Socrates, one of the founding fathers of the university, was a master provocateur. I like to have open discussion in my classroom, and I don't try to have the last word. My job is not to make students think what I think. My job is primarily to get them thinking methodically. But my classroom has a goal of truth—not thinking for thinking's sake. Socrates provoked discussion in order to move toward the truth. If you find yourself in a provocative classroom, use the discussion to help you pursue truth— even if the professor seems to have no concern about where the discussion goes.

Understanding Your Teachers

Another thing: don't expect faculty at universities to be "normal." All faculty are a bit eccentric and some very eccentric. By the mere fact that they were willing to be graduate students for a long time in order to have the chance of attaining a low-paying job, they are abnormal beings.

Every campus does have a few stylish profs who dazzle with good looks and sophistication. They look all the more beautiful and sophisticated because most of us look a bit disheveled and clumsy. On prestigious campuses you will find famous professors such as John Kenneth Galbraith, a handsome Harvard economist who from the 1940s to the present has led a jet-set life with the American and European aristocracy. Galbraith regularly gets calls from the White House and national news programs, all the while being charming, brilliant and witty. Recently appointed as a dean at Stanford is Condoleezza Rice, a beautiful expert in Soviet military affairs, who in serving the presidential administrations of the 1980s, speaking at the Republican National Convention and appearing often on television seems every bit as charming, brilliant and witty as Galbraith.

Most professors, however, are neither glamorous nor witty. Lots of them have unsocial quirks. I read once about a professor who put a chalkboard in his dining room so that he could better lecture his family and any visitors. Usually professors would rather be in a library or a laboratory than talking in public. Some are scared and inhibited when they stand in front of a class, while others can lecture confidently but are very shy with an individual student.

My wife complains that professors often give complex answers to simple questions. As a student, she was walking to class with a professor one day and ventured to ask him whether he was a Christian. He gave a long answer, but when they parted she was not sure whether he thought he was or wasn't.

Every college student has some stories of professors to tell. When I was a graduate student, one of my professors invited my wife and me to a large formal party. The food was catered. Tablecloths were brilliant white. The chancellor's wife wore long earrings and a fancy gown. My wife nudged my arm when the host walked into the room with his white shirttail sticking out of his fly. She wanted me to go and tell him to zip up, but before I could his wife grabbed him and dragged him into the kitchen. He quickly reappeared fully zipped. Such is a fancy occasion with faculty.

My most eccentric professor chain-smoked cigarettes under the classroom "No Smoking" sign. He was fidgety and nervous when teaching. He would write one word on the blackboard and then pound the end of his chalk on the word for the next hour. Many of us never took our eyes off him, because we were sure that any minute he was going to pound his cigarette on the word while shoving the chalk into his mouth. Every once in a while he would knock over his podium, spilling his lecture notes across the floor. A year later an acquaintance who was taking the class figured out that the professor knocked the podium over only when he was asked hard questions about something he didn't know much about. The professor probably did it unconsciously; however, my acquaintance and some coconspirators plotted a series of questions to figure out which type would send the lecture notes flying. By the end of the course, the students could send the lecture notes flying almost at will.

Almost all faculty have personality quirks and ugly clothes that you will scrutinize for two or three hours a week. Get past them and realize that you have the rare opportunity of being able to interact with highly trained people who have thought long and hard on a subject. Professors usually love their subjects. Even when engulfed in boring subjects, professors always have much to offer.

At state schools, we professors are paid by your taxes and your tuition to talk to you. We are paid to help you. Most of us will bend over backwards to help a student who is hardworking and interested in gaining an education. Accept our failings and use us as a resource. Compare what we say with your own experience and what you already know. Compare it with what other professors have said and with what your parents, church and friends have taught you. Confront us with your intellectual struggles. We can help.

Faculty are not always right. We are knowledgeable but often not wise. Don't expect too much from us. But understand that to go through college without developing a close relationship with at least one professor would be a major failure on your part. To not have at least one professor who knows you by name means you have not even begun to tap the resources of the university.

One of my friends, Bill Rumsey, is a tall, chain-smoking, fiftysomething philosophy professor who, with his long, wild, graying hair, looks like Charlton Heston as Moses. He is not a Christian and is absolutely committed to teaching the intricacies of thinking and pursuit of precision. Students don't rush to fill his classes. Aristotle, Plato and Aquinas are included on the reading lists. You don't read *about* those thinkers. You actually read *them*. My friend is a tough, uncompromising and imposing professor. He loves his students too much to give them anything less.

Last year a mutual student of ours was having a rough time. He was emotionally unstable and not thinking rigorously about a lot of bad philosophy that he was reading. Several times he talked to us about suicide. Late one afternoon the student's girlfriend came to Rumsey, sure that her boyfriend was going to kill himself. Rumsey went looking for the student and found him walking across the campus. The next day the student told me that he was starting a new research project with Rumsey.

Being a professor is a high calling of close interaction between individuals. At many universities you will initially be placed in huge classes where the professor wears a microphone and stands on a stage. From this distance the professor will seem incredibly important and busy. Don't let the situation block you from seeking one-on-one discussion. Every professor has office hours for students. It's up to you to visit the professor during office hours and show him or her that you are more than just an FTE (Full Time Equivalent) statistic.

Most professors will react favorably. Almost all professors want to talk to students. A professor nearing retirement once told me that talking to students made him feel young. Most professors are happiest when trying to help a student.

Wisdom and Knowledge

Almost all professors have spent at least four to six years in graduate school after four or five years as an undergraduate. Most of them earn a Ph.D. (some business people earn a D.B.A., most education professors earn an Ed.D., arts professors most often have an M.F.A.). "Ph.D." stands for *doctor of philosophy: doctor* coming from the Latin for "teacher" and *philosophy* from the Greek for "love of wisdom." Ten or more years of higher education is suppose to make a person able to teach the love of wisdom. There is a problem here. Graduate schools do not teach the love of wisdom. The Ph.D. actually signifies extensive knowledge, not love of wisdom.

Wisdom and knowledge are very different. Wisdom is much bigger and more practical. Wisdom is the ability to make decisions that lead to a better life, a better society, a better world. Wisdom is a gift of God. Paul calls Jesus the wisdom of God. The fruits of the Spirit—love, joy, peace, patience, kindness, goodness, fidelity, gentleness and self-control—are aspects of wisdom. Knowledge is less practical. Knowledge is information that is stored and retrieved but not necessarily put into practice. Knowers are not always servants. Wise people are always servants.

Knowledge has little to do with love. In 1 Corinthians 8:1, " 'knowledge' inflates a man, whereas love builds him up," and in 1 Corinthians 13:8, knowledge will "vanish" and love will prevail. You will find that many knowledgeable Christians are not wise and certainly not loving. You will also find that God has showered many non-Christians with wisdom and given them hearts full of love.

At secular universities, all the faculty have much knowledge and some are wise. The wisest professors I know were not hired at the university for their wisdom—they were hired because they had lots of knowledge. That they are wise is a bonus that the university got by chance.

Search out the wise professors. Search out the classes that honor the love of wisdom. Some of your best professors will not be Christians, and some of your best classes might even be antagonistic to Christianity. Many wise professors have been affected by a modern culture that no longer takes the Bible seriously and where the devil has been wily in making Christianity look foolish. Wisdom does not mean perfection. As for yourself, pray for wisdom along with increased knowledge.

To find the best professors and classes, just ask around. The student body of every college has a fairly accurate informal network of information about classes and professors. But always remember that the majority of college students, like the majority of people in society, just want to get by the easiest way possible. As a Christian, you have a responsibility to seek out the best education and think hard about the information presented to you in classes. Christians are called to the narrow path, not the wide road. God has given you a great opportunity to be in college among smart people who are trying to understand our world to the best of their ability. From the one to whom much is given, much is expected. As in the parable of the talents, God demands that you invest in the opportunity of education that you have been given.

Christian Fellowship on Campus

Much of the educational life on campus is based around meetings with professors; however, lots of it is not. As a member of the university you have membership in a community of students. Students often learn more from each other than they learn from professors. In campus clubs and informal after-class meetings in the cafeteria you can learn as much as or more than in your classes. Wisdom to use knowledge well is best learned in fellowship with other students in campus activities.

Christians should be among the most vigorous members of the university community. The university is as much our place as anyone else's. On the newspaper staff, in student government or in the poetry club, you have much to offer and gain.

Aside from those activities, it is also important that you join with Christian clubs or informal groups. Christians have a subculture in America. A subculture is a good thing. Immigrant groups, political loyalists, theater lovers and even followers of the Grateful Dead have subcultures with their own institutions, organizations, books, magazines, bumper stickers and computer networks to support them. The Greek system of fraternities and sororities is a type of subculture. Every active American probably belongs to several subcultures. They help us commune with kindred spirits and dig deeper into the meaning of what draws us together, and they strengthen our ability to affect the larger culture. We serious Christians, as opposed to merely nominal Christians, have our books, music and magazines, but our fellowship organizations may be the most important aspect of our subculture. Jesus tells us that wherever two or three are gathered, he will be there.

He is there for the one, of course, but he probably said "two or three" in order to encourage us to form fellowship groups.

Most universities will have a number of Christian fellowship groups to choose from. The Roman Catholics have Newman Centers. The Episcopalians have Canterbury Houses. Southern Baptists have organizations with various names. Protestant evangelicals have such groups as InterVarsity, Navigators and Campus Crusade for Christ.

During my first year of college at a polytechnic university in San Luis Obispo I shopped around for a fellowship group. A friend took me to the Navigators. They emphasized memorizing Bible verses and doing heavy Bible study. I liked them. They were rigorous. But something about them wasn't my style. So I checked out InterVarsity. They had more emphasis on fun and still had good Bible studies. (InterVarsity people lovingly called the Navigators the "Never-Daters.") InterVarsity was the largest Christian organization on campus—but a little too large for my taste. I eventually only hung out on the edge of both the Navigators and InterVarsity. I became involved in an informal Christian group that met for Bible study at one of the dormitories on Sunday nights. I think the campus InterVarsity leader encouraged our formation and offered indirect support, but we students ran the whole thing on our own. The women I dated, the friends I looked for at lunchtime and, in general, the people who made me feel more than a number at the university were in that group.

I favor ad hoc fellowship groups—informal clubs of a few friends who band together for mutual improvement. They can be study groups that meet for one semester to help members understand a class or regular breakfast get-togethers at which two or three agree to meet for a purpose, whether to discuss theological topics or to pray or to study the Bible. Such groups, as they come and go, can easily become one of the most important aspects of your college life.

A famous old handbook for young adults called *The Compleat Gentleman* recommends not studying too much since too much solitary bookwork can stifle your spirit. *The Compleat Gentleman* recommends taking daily walks full of pleasant discussion and mutual refreshment with compatriots.

I have studied the lives of students at Harvard College around 1700. One of my favorite stories is of Dutch tourists who walked from Boston on a hot, dusty day to see the little college of fewer than a hundred students. As they approached they saw no one but heard boisterous clamoring from the second floor of an undistinguished brick hall. They climbed the stairs and opened the door into a room clouded with pipe smoke. A group of Harvard's best students were having a raucous time practicing debates. No one in authority was around. The students were on their own, having fun while joining together for mutual improvement. Among the students were future ministers, teachers at Harvard and founders of Yale College.

At Oxford University a few decades later, John Wesley, his brother Charles and George Whitefield gathered with others in a "Holy Club" of prayer and Bible study. These men went on to lead a great revival of Christianity in England and America. The founding of the Methodist Church is sometimes traced through the Wesleys back to that college fellowship group.

Don't forget that you might include a professor in your fellowship group. Alexander Campbell Fraser tells a story of an informal group formed with a professor. As a student at the University of Edinburgh in the 1830s, Fraser enrolled in a course on metaphysics taught by William Hamilton. (Metaphysics is a wonderful part of philosophy that studies the mind, soul and other nonphysical aspects of nature. Metaphysics deals with the "ultimate questions" with which Christians are always concerned.) As sometimes happens to good teachers, Hamilton got in trouble for not filling out the right forms, and the administration eventually canceled his metaphysics course. Hamilton kept up an informal study group discussing metaphysics at his house in the evenings. Fraser, who later became a professor of logic and metaphysics at Edinburgh, remembered those informal evenings as a turning point in his life. He wrote, "I owe more to Hamilton than to any other intellectual influence."

College education is meant to be collegial—in groups. Pursuing knowledge is hard going when you go it alone. Find some friends with similar interests. Stake out a booth at some pizza place one night a week. Where five or six regularly gather for discussing important subjects, there shall be college life at its best. "It is in them," wrote a proponent of small informal groups, "that a general college life is chiefly nourished." Over a century ago this proponent rightly pointed out that "the variety of topics of discussion and essay keep the minds of [students] in freer and broader action than is possible in the pursuit of purely academical studies." Freer and broader! That is what Christians students need most! Christian students need the wide-open, full-throttle and conscientiously introspective search for truth that is not usually possible within the limitations of "purely academical studies."

In a later chapter I will explain the basic limitations of academical studies. Right now I have only one bit of advice: Start or join a small group that can change your life.

Church Fellowship

Campus fellowship groups are important, but they become a problem when students use them as substitutes for churches. Churches are the fundamental organizations of Christianity. The book of Acts is the account of the founding of the church. Churches administer the sacraments. They marry people and nurture families. Churches are the bride of Christ and the true fellowship of believers. Never confuse a campus fellowship group with the fellowship of believers that is a church.

Two churches supported me in my first two years of college in San Luis Obispo. University bureaucrats lost my dorm application, so I was without campus housing when I started college. My older brother got me a room in a decrepit boarding house owned by a very small Four Square Gospel charismatic church. That church considered it part of its outreach to supply inexpensive housing to a dozen or so folk. The people of the church watched over the building and us in a very kind way, and I am sure they prayed vigorously for us. I was part of part of their social and campus outreach. This is one of the great aspects of being part of our Christian subculture: people who have nothing to gain from us are often watching out for us.

I visited the Four Square church at times, but I regularly attended a Nazarene church where I helped lead the youth groups. The Four Square and Nazarene churches were very different from the Presbyterian church I grew up in, but each took care of me.

In every college town there are churches that have a special calling to minister to college students who are away from families and their hometown churches. Look for them. I am confident that the prayers of the Four Square Gospelers and the Nazarenes in San Luis Obispo, as they asked God to watch over the minds of the college students entrusted to them, availed much in my life.

Fellowship groups and churches are also good bases for serving. The fact that you are a student does not mean that you have no responsibility to serve the university, your community, your church, your nation and the world. Get involved. An old monastic adage is "Work is prayer." Washing dishes at the local homeless shelter, teaching Sunday school, even pushing for political reform are the kinds of service to which Christians are called.

College church groups and fellowship groups should be unified in study, prayer and work. The devil wants to make us narrowly focused. Jesus wants us to be, like him, a light in the world. Get involved.

— 4 —

The Pursuit
of Truth
A Circle
& a Race

Your highest goal at college is to seek first the kingdom of God, to love the Lord your God with all your heart, mind and strength, and to learn more of God's truth. You have a foundation of knowledge in your mind: you have experienced God and the gift of joy and love. You know God has a purpose for creation. You don't fully understand, but you know in the depths of your being that you are created in the image of God, that you are a spiritual being as much as or more than you are a physical being. You have a conscience that is somehow a conduit for knowing right and wrong.

You know much already; however, more knowledge requires your active pursuit. The fullness of truth is infinitely beyond our finite minds, yet universities throughout history have been good places for catching glimmers of new light from God. The reason God has blessed universities in this way partly has to do with two essential methods of learning that universities support. The two can be pictured using the images of a circle and a race. One is a circle because we learn from each other, including from those long dead. We hold hands in a circle, learning from each other; the university is a place of communal learning. But the second image is a race because we run, full of ambition, alone in our lane, toward a goal.

Wait. Have I created contradictory metaphors? How can one hold hands in a circle of people while racing alone toward a finish line? Good point, but the fact of contradiction doesn't mean that you are not supposed to be doing both at the same time. Such is the tension in the best learning. Pursuit of truth requires succeeding at the hard job of being in a circle and a race at the same time.

The Communion of Truth-Seekers

First, the circle. I take the image from the old gospel song:

Will the circle be unbroken
By and by, Lord, by and by?
There's a better home awaiting
In the sky, Lord, in the sky.

The song is about the funeral of the singer's mother and the singer's question and affirmation that the family is not broken up by death. The song is also an affirmation of the "communion of saints" spoken of in the Apostles' Creed. The unbroken fellowship is the ultimate fellowship of all Christians—past, present and future.

As Christians at a university we do not think alone. Our minds are not simply personal property, and our mental skills are not so great that one person can decide or know everything. We learn by wise trusting. Some professors, textbooks and even other students gain our trust, and we then believe what they tell us. God is also communicating with us—especially through the Bible and our churches. We must trust the Bible and our churches as much as or more than we trust our professors and textbooks.

Since creation God has desired to communicate with humanity. Humanity in the Fall of Adam and Eve severely messed up the communication. But God is still communicating. The Bible is the Word of God. It is a specific and authoritative revelation given through prophets and apostles. The Holy Spirit also reveals knowledge to churches and individual Christians. God has communicated much truth through time to the whole communion of saints, the whole circle of Christians. God's wisdom is especially allotted in bits to individuals throughout time. Accumulated wisdom requires assembling the wisdom of individuals into a larger whole. Do not think that you, with your lone mind, are charged with discovering all God's truth by yourself or with making wise choices on the basis of your own meager wisdom. Christian learning is not rugged individualism. Christian learning is holding hands in an unbroken circle listening to each other and to God. The whole is greater than any part. Christian learning is ultimately corporate prayer that is answered at different times and in measured amounts to various members of the circle.

A recent book by an Australian philosopher, *Testimony* by C. A. J. Coady, is about how the advance of learning in universities is based more on everyone in universities listening to and trusting each other than on individuals doing their individual research. Universities are productive because they bring people together in a situation where people can listen and trust each other. This is true for everyone—scientists, historians, mathematicians, psychologists, everyone. Coady condemns the common image of the lone researcher against the world discovering something that is new. Universities are built on simple trust. Honesty is the institution's highest value, because without honest communication the project of inquiry is destroyed.

Non-Christians and Christians alike must listen and trust in order to pursue knowledge. We all must hold hands with our colleagues and our predecessors. All scholars must hold hands with all scholars, but Christians have a special calling to hold hands with those who are not necessarily scholars. Christians seek the wisdom that God showers in bits on everyone—rich, poor, young, old, educated, uneducated, mystic in a monastery, evangelist on TV. Most importantly, Christians trust the doctrines taught in the Bible and confirmed by the communion of saints over the last two thousand years.

The modern university has the problem of teaching too much individualism and not enough hand-holding. G. K. Chesterton, a wonderful writer, described our duty as thinkers as a broad form of democracy—everybody should get a vote in what we think. Some may tell you that this is not being "true to yourself" or even that it is not "honest," but I believe that overemphasis on individualism in learning is the devil's most wily and destructive tool in modern society.

Running to Win

Individualism, however, has its proper role after you realize that we all must put our trust in a circle of trustworthy people from the past and the present. Remember Paul's description of the race? "At the games, as you know, all the runners take part, though only one wins the prize. You also must run to win. Every athlete goes into strict training. They do it to win a fading garland; we, to win a garland that never fades" (1 Cor 9:24-25).

God calls us to the race, to be runners. The unbroken circle is not just a homogenization of everything everybody has ever thought, so that the runner is tripping over everybody's feet while holding their hands. God calls us as individuals. God calls each of us to individual judgment and discernment. God demands an individual ambition to follow the path to truth wherever it leads, to run a race for an eternal prize.

Ambition is crucial. Lots of books on the progress of science emphasize the competitive nature of good scholars. Read *The Double Helix,* by James D. Watson and Francis Crick, a classic account of the race to discover the structure of DNA. Read G. H. Hardy's *A Mathematician's Apology,* which declares that "ambition is the driving force behind nearly all the best work in the world." Watson, Crick and Hardy are three of the great minds among twentieth-century academics who understand that competition and ambition are important in universities. Paul warns against racing for an unworthy prize; however, self-discipline, training and desire to win are the characteristics he and most modern academics advocate for pursuers of truth.

As a student you are striving for the prize of knowledge and wisdom. As a Christian student you are striving for God's truth, and you must be individually ambitious. You must be filled with desire. You must will yourself to work. Learning is not passive. It is not like eating a meal. Learning is a race. The winners have discipline, ambition and a will that propels them to their highest for the utmost.

A long-held principle in the communion of saints is that your desires affect your rationality. The philosopher John Locke stated the principle concisely: "He that would seriously set upon the search for truth, ought in the first place to prepare his mind with the love of it. For he that loves it not, will not take much pains to get it; nor be much concerned when he misses it."

Your life at the university is a serious and exciting life. Love God, love your neighbor. Join a church, pray and study with others. Seek out the good classes and the good professors. Don't let the knowledge industry get in the way of being a member of a society pursuing knowledge. Remember that you are weakest when you think and act as a loner. Join hands with others in the unbroken circle which God has blessed with knowledge and wisdom throughout history. Trust one another. Have ambition, run the race, strive for the right prize.

Individually, there is no greater discipline than beginning each day with reading the Bible and prayer. It is the discipline of those who are ambitious for God. It is a discipline that encourages humility and love, since it is a way to hold hands with Jesus, the apostles and the biblical members of our circle. Such a discipline can help turn knowledge into wisdom.

— 5 —

University Values
Rationality, Increasing Knowledge & Unity

All American universities have a Christian foundation. Their mottoes are filled with the language of God. Harvard's motto used to be *In gloriam Christi* ("for the glory of Christ"), and *veritas* ("truth") is still inscribed on its seal. The Indiana University seal states that *lux et veritas,* "light and truth," are our goals. The University of California's seal is inscribed with God's command in Genesis 1: "Let there be light!" More recently, mottoes have given way to mission statements. At secular universities these statements no longer mention Christ or quote the Bible, yet they still easily fit a Christian foundation and purpose. Here, for example, is the mission statement written in the 1980s for the commuter university I teach at:

> Indiana University Southeast embraces the traditional goals of liberal education: intellectual development and the stimulation and perpetuation of a spirit of free inquiry directed toward an under-

standing of humanity and the universe. Realization of these high
purposes is served by activities designed to increase knowledge;
develop the ability to reason; enlarge and deepen aesthetic sensi-
tivity; deal intelligently with moral and spiritual questions, social
issues, and scientific and technological problems; assist students in
identifying their aptitudes, enhancing their abilities and broadening
their interests; and foster the development of character which
embraces the highest ideals.

No Christian should have a problem with that mission. Our job in the
university is simply to claim our right to be included as part of the
mission. This mission statement was written so as not to exclude any
specific religious form of rationality. If it allows for Buddhism,
Marxism or Freudianism, it also allows for Christianity. In fact, we
can thrive within such a mission statement.

The Separation of Church and State

Read the mission statement again. First, it affirms a tradition that goes
back to the Middle Ages and further back to Greek, Jewish and early
Christian foundations. Second, it baldly states that universities deal,
in part, with spiritual questions. Finally, the issues and problems faced
are of as much interest to Christians as they are to anyone trying to
help society.

Sure: church and state are supposedly separate in the United States.
Universities that rely on public funds cannot be specifically committed to one religion. They must be pluralistic. Christians shouldn't want
it to be any other way at tax-supported institutions. We live in a
pluralistic country, and our institutions must reflect and embrace that
pluralism. That is what loving one's neighbor is partly about. Many
Christians are involved in running secular universities and have a
responsibility to allow those universities to support the perspectives
of their neighbors, just as they must allow those universities to support
the perspectives of their fellow church members. Christians of every
persuasion certainly have the right to create and run specifically
Christian universities; however, they do not have the right to run them

with taxes taken from people who do not support Christianity. Let Christians pay for their own institutions. Without the strings attached to government money, Christian institutions can have more integrity. Where taxes are used, pluralism must reign. As Americans we recognize the fundamental right that our taxes should serve the people as a whole, not one specific religious perspective.

The separation of church and state, however, does not mean that religions cannot be an important part of public education. Church and state both strive for the good, the just, the moral and the true. Education must strive to embrace the wholeness of existence. The principal meaning of separation of church and state is that no one church will be institutionally favored and that the government will not rule over an individual's religious conscience. Thomas Jefferson, in the introduction to his bill for establishing religious freedom in Virginia, declared two of our country's great ideals: "that our civil rights have no dependence on our religious opinions" and "that the truth is great and will prevail if left to herself; that she is the proper and sufficient antagonist to error, and has nothing to fear from the conflict unless by human interposition disarmed of her natural weapons, free argument and debate."

Truth is a power. Truth prevails where freedom of thought is encouraged. You and I cannot box in truth, and we cannot protect it from a world full of error. Truth does not need us. We need it. We believe that Christianity has the widest and best understanding of truth; however, truth isn't limited to Christianity. The American separation of church and state is meant to allow truth and religion wide freedom in public institutions. The separation of church and state does not remove Christianity from universities; rather, it frees Christianity from the possibility of corruption and imposition from the state.

So, even though Christianity is not favored at public universities, it can thrive there, especially since those universities still pursue the ideals of good, justice, morality and truth. Not only are Christian goals the same as university goals, the methods of pursuing the goals are similar. The traditional idea of a university is founded on the ultimate unity of truth, the ability of human reason to increase knowledge and the importance of sharing knowledge in order to construct a body of knowledge greater than any one person's knowledge. These are Christian values as much as they are the university's.

Universities and Tradition

Of course the traditional ideas of a university are constantly being debated. Some of your professors will declare that human reason is hopelessly flawed or even just an illusion. Many might hold that the only one truth is that there is no one truth. Some may even go so far as to say there is no such thing as intellectual communication between humans, that a reader can't know what an author is saying and therefore that knowledge cannot accumulate or increase.

Such things were told me by a candidate desiring to be hired as a new English professor. I asked the candidate if her beliefs meant that she wouldn't strive to teach with rationally organized lectures or grade papers by college standards or write articles for academic journals. I asked how she handled a contradiction in a student's paper. (If you try to resolve contradictions, it implies to some extent a belief in pursuing unified communication and truth.) In every case the candidate started retreating—usually saying that the theories could be true but the classroom required something more pragmatic than theories.

We offered her the job. Universities need diverse ideas. Most of us on the interviewing committee believe (explicitly or implicitly) that truth will win out in the long run. The traditional ideas of a university usually do win over the antitraditional ideas because the structure of universities and the reason they exist support the traditional ideas. Universities by their very existence—by their emphasis on resolving scientific or logical contradictions, by their emphasis on rating the quality of student work according to standards, by their emphasis on scholarly publication—declare the Christian values of rationality, increasing knowledge and unified truth. The *uni* in *university* is still the ideal: rationality increasing knowledge toward a greater unity.

Too many Christian students act as if they are in enemy territory on campus. They treat their campus Christian activities as covert operations. Certainly committed Christians are a minority on university campuses just as they are in society; however, they should not feel like undercover agents. The central assertion of this book is that the Christian has got home-court advantage at a public university. In the contest against the devil, the university is a playing field or court where the Christians have the advantage of both tradition and the stated ideals and mottoes. It is one of the devil's wiles to make Christians think of universities as enemy territory. Love the university. Wherever the goal is knowledge and truth, there is a place for Christians. The devil is the one on enemy territory and is the covert agent.

I first heard that a student could love the university after I transferred to the University of California at Santa Barbara (UCSB), a school not as famous as its sisters at Los Angeles and Berkeley but much nicer, since it is built on a beach rather than in a city. At that time UCSB had approximately fifteen thousand students. I lived frugally one block from campus and one block from the beach in a two-bedroom apartment with four other guys, three of whom were Christians active in InterVarsity Christian Fellowship. Our apartment became a sort of clubhouse for a group of hard-core religious studies majors and Christian students who wanted to debate, argue, yell and pound their fists over any theological/intellectual question that passed by. For a while, some friends created an ad hoc seminar on Christianity and the university. We would invite religiously oriented university professors to our apartment on Sunday afternoons for some intellectual wrestling.

The Sunday-afternoon professor I remember most was Raimundo Panikkar. He came to tell us we must love the university. He was revered by many students and other professors. He was rumored to know gobs of foreign languages and to have three Ph.D. degrees. He was, among other things, a Roman Catholic priest, who sometimes preached at the historic mission church downtown. At our Sunday meeting he entered our apartment wearing sandals and the flowing white robes of his native country. He was followed by what looked like disciples. Our living room was packed, with everyone on the floor except for Panikkar, who sat cross-legged on the couch with a large window behind him. The backlighting made his long white hair glow. He talked to us with a soft voice about how the university was like a church, a place close to God where a community of scholars reaches out for knowledge, understanding and wisdom.

I think he was mostly wrong. The church is the bride of Christ and is the place where the sacraments are offered. The church is the true fellowship of believers and is spiritually and intellectually much bigger and more important than universities. But Panikkar was doing the right thing to make us think about our lives at the university as part of our sacred lives as Christians. He wanted us to embrace our classes and homework as Christian work. He wanted us to long for truth like the psalmist longed for God:

As a deer longs for the running streams,

so I long for you, my God.

I thirst for God, the living God. (Ps 42:1-2)

Panikkar taught us that the university is a gift from God to humanity. It is a special place for those longing and thirsting for God. He was right about that.

Western Civilization and Universities

To say that the idea of an American university is Christian will raise loud objections from some. Christians need to be careful to explain what they mean in such situations. American universities are "Christian" because they are rooted in a Western Christian tradition built on ancient Greek and Hebrew foundations revised and modified by Christianity. Judeo-Christian monotheism is at the root of the university's traditional belief in the ultimate oneness of knowledge: a unity which justifies joining all the varieties of knowledge and strategies for attaining knowledge into one *uni*versity. Judeo-Christian monotheism is the belief in one God, a Creator God in whom all knowledge and rationalism is unified. That Creator God also organizes creation; therefore, humans can increase knowledge by studying the patterns and order in the universe. (Eastern civilization is largely rooted in religions or philosophies such as Buddhism, Taoism and Confucianism, which have no personal Creator God who unifies and empowers truth.)

The mentality of a Western university is also rooted in Islam, because Islam is rooted in Judeo-Christian monotheism. The God of Abraham, the God of Truth who reaches out to communicate with humanity, is the God of all three religions. In the early Middle Ages the Muslims built the first great centers of education and research. European universities learned some of their rational methods from Islam.

Note also that all three religions have a sacred text which the young are taught to analyze. One aspect of your home-court advantage is that Christians who have grown up going to Sunday school and listening to sermons have an advantage in college over those who grew up watching TV on Sunday mornings. Jews and Muslims have similar educational experiences and also do well in college. Christian, Jewish and Muslim youth are taught to read carefully, analyze relationships between passages and apply what was written to larger problems. They also regularly hear rational presentations on learned topics. In my classes I am always happy to have religious fundamentalists from all three religions because they often are my best students.

While on the subject of Jews and Muslims, always remember that we Christians have much in common with other religious-minded people seriously committed to understanding God's role in the cosmos. Of course we have crucial differences—one crucial difference is Jesus. In love, however, remember that as a member of a campus Christian club you have more in common with the members of the campus Jewish clubs than with members of nonreligious clubs.

The Christian Roots of Universities

One of the core ideas shared by Judaism, Islam and Christianity is that humanity was created in the image of God. The creation story we share tells us so. Throughout history most Christians have interpreted this to mean that humans were made with immortal souls and rationality. Rationality involves a complex interaction of reason, affections, memories, intuition and innate knowledge. Universities were created to encourage the image of God in us so that university graduates might better serve God and society. Universities were funded and continue to be funded as social investments where teachers, students, governments and taxpayers deposit their resources in the hope of a high return. In Jesus' parable of the talents one servant invested his talents well and they increased, another less well but they still increased, while a third buried the talent, making no investment or increase. The parable demands that we invest the talent of rationality that God has given us. Universities are our best investment houses.

Jesus tells us that from the one to whom much is given much is expected. We who have been given the talent of rationality are expected to invest it. From those to whom God has given the opportunity of attending a university much is expected.

Our universities are not only a product of religion; they are also a product of a culture which is called Western civilization. This civilization developed out of the western and northern portion of the Roman Empire. (Christianity is larger than Western civilization. Our religion also spread eastward and southward from the Mediterranean. In those directions Christian societies had a tougher time than in the northwest.) When the Roman Empire's bureaucracy began to fall apart, education in Rome and Europe was kept alive by the Christian churches. Greece and Rome had developed a strong system of liberal arts that included logic and mathematics. Christians adopted the liberal arts since they had proven themselves to be useful tools.

Paul had gone to the Greeks and used their rationalistic skills in order to convert them. Christ welcomed Gentiles. God revealed to Peter that Christianity was to extend beyond Judaism. The Greeks had been non-Christians, but Paul and the later church leaders who created universities saw that many of the Greeks had been honest and ardent pursuers of the truth. Later church leaders could even see similarities to Christianity in the writings of the great philosophers Plato and

Aristotle. It seemed clear that God had at least partially answered some of the Greeks' questions before coming in human form to the Jews. Paul and the majority of church leaders felt led by the Holy Spirit to adopt some of the rational skills of the Greeks and install them into Christian education and thinking.

Christian Rationalism

The Jews and Christians knew very well that there was a danger in education. Pride can infect knowledge. Also, since rationality is a complex mixture of reason, affections, memories and inborn knowledge, the mixture can easily get out of balance in fallen humans, resulting in skewed rationality. The apostle Paul in his letters warned against overemphasizing knowledge. Tertullian, one of the early fathers of the church, tried to discourage Christians from adopting the rational tools of Greeks by asking, "What does Athens have to do with Jerusalem?" This is a famous sound bite in Christian history but is not a good argument. Paul and Peter never insisted that Jerusalem had nothing to do with Athens. Tertullian himself used Greek rational tools to further the work of Christ.

A more subtle approach to the relationship of Greek rational tools to the young Christian church was offered by Origen, one of the greatest thinkers among the early church fathers. Origen likened Greek rational tools to the spoils that the Jews took with them from Egypt in the exodus. Of course the spoils were "the wisdom of this world" and "the wealth of sinners"; nonetheless, they were useful and could be made more useful when touched by God. Origen offered another biblical image: Greek rational tools were like the Philistine women in Genesis 20:17-18 who were unable to bear children until Abraham asked God to heal them. Avoiding the oversimplification of men such as Tertullian, Origen advised prayerful and wise assimilation of the good tools of Greek rationalism.

Origen understood that the Bible is both simple and complex. It teaches plain literal facts, such as the historical fact that Christ died on the cross and rose from the dead. But Origen also understood that

God interweaves parts of the Bible into larger wholes. For example, the meaning of Jesus' death and resurrection is more fully understood when put in the context of Moses raising a serpent on a staff and of Isaiah's image of a lamb going to slaughter.

Origen was adamant about the authority of Holy Scriptures as both plain and complex revelation from God. He insisted that in matters of great importance—such as understanding our souls or the cosmic battle between God and the devil—Christians must rely on the authority of Holy Scripture more than on Greek logic. Origen carefully distinguished what we know from our own logic and what we know directly from God. The two were not contradictory, but the former could easily go awry and mislead Christians.

Maybe most important for those of us who watch Christians fight each other over the less important matters of Christianity, Origen taught Greek distinctions between incontrovertible demonstration and lesser forms of knowledge. There are some things that are clearly and distinctly taught by God and proven from the Bible. But there are many Christian doctrines and ideas that are logical speculations derived from the Bible or the innate knowledge we have from God. Origen was always careful to distinguish his demonstrable conclusions from his speculations. Demonstrations "compel assent," whereas speculations allow for disagreement. The greatest Christian thinkers in history have also been careful to make this distinction, which was originally derived from the Greeks. Paul himself makes such distinctions. Paul received direct revelations from God, but he also speculated. In 1 Corinthians he speculates about the role of apostles in the end times (4:9); he makes "concessions not commands" (7:6); and when giving marriage advice, he writes "as my own word, not as the Lord's" (7:12). There are doctrines we have received from God which demand assent, but we Christians also have speculations which we are free to pray about, work through and discuss over pizza.

Origen died in A.D. 253 after being tortured for his faith. Would that you and I could be described in the same way he is by a modern scholar: "He loved truth with a sincerity and devotion rarely equalled, and never excelled. . . . The wide sweep of his thought is amazing. He contemplated a universe, not small and narrow as was that of many of his contemporaries, but of immense magnitude."

Careful and wise assimilation of Greek rational tools like Origen's became the hope of the early church. Assimilation was needed if Christians were to offer an answer to fundamental questions of our religion.

Rational Tools and the Trinity

The existence of the Trinity was one of the most fundamental questions that Christians had to work out. That God is One is clearly an Old Testament principle: "The Lord our God is one" (Deut 6:4). However, in Jesus' words and in the writings that were becoming the New Testament there were many references to a Creator/Father God, a Holy Spirit and a God the Son. And the divinity of Jesus as the Son was indicated by such things as his virgin birth and many of his statements—for example, "The Father and I are one" (Jn 10:30). The One God was clearly complex, and some sort of threeness in the One God was evident. As the Scriptures were collected together the problem was not cleared up. Jesus and the authors of the New Testament did not discuss the threeness, nor did any scriptural passage exist where the Father, Son and Holy Spirit were shown working side by side.

Much prayer and discussion went into what was a rational problem. God did not offer a revelation as an answer. God, for some purpose, often chooses not to give simple revelations as answers to our questions. Instead he gives us tools such as our reason. God also supplies us help in more subtle ways than direct revelation, such as the winds of the Holy Spirit and, apparently, the intervention of angels and other spiritual beings. In the situation of an intellectual problem such as the Trinity, God supplied the help we needed but demanded our use of Greek logic to supply definitions and categories such as *person, being, substance* and *equality.* Church leaders, over the course of more than a hundred years, gathered at various meetings and two major church councils and there used Greek definitions and categories to discuss the problem. Trusting in the Holy Spirit's guidance, the leaders of Christianity decided on an answer: the Trinity.

There is still debate on the Trinity, but the important point is that the Jewish doctrine of the Oneness of God and the New Testament's presentation of Jesus and the Holy Spirit as deity were synthesized by Christians relying on Greek rationalism and the help of the Holy Spirit. Greek categories of substance and personness offered a way that 1 = 3 could be rational while on the whole still remaining a mystery.

At this point I should explain an important situation in the Bible that today affects discussion of the Trinity and also shows Greek rationalism at work. If you look in a modern Bible at 1 John 5:7-8, you will probably find an odd little glitch in the numbering, or maybe a footnote. If you have a King James Version, you will find a clear passage describing the Trinity as the three that testify: the Father, Son (or Word) and Holy Spirit. Almost all newer versions of the Bible do not have this passage and only list the three testifiers as spirit, water and blood. The story of this passage is important.

About five hundred years ago some Christian scholars, comparing old manuscripts of the Bible with newer ones, found that the newer ones had the Trinity passage in 1 John but that *all* of the old ones did not. So a question presented itself: Which are the more correct Bibles? What would you decide? Here's another clue: in *all* of the oldest books discussing the Trinity, *nowhere* is the 1 John passage used to prove the existence of the Trinity. So which is the more correct Bible?

Logic and methods of thinking developed by the Greeks helped those Christians five hundred years ago decide that the most correct Bibles were the ones that did not include the Trinity verse in 1 John. They reasoned that early in the Middle Ages the short little passage on the Trinity was added into the Bible. It was probably first added by a monk who was trying to explain to himself or his friends what the spirit, water and blood symbolized. Over the years, many more Bibles included the monk's little addition. Today most Bibles do not have the passage. This is one way that rationalism helps us keep our Christianity more pure, with fewer human errors.

Love, Humility and Rationalism

Some early Christians and Jews balked at using Greek logic in Christianity, and there continues to be a minority of Christians who try to avoid the taint of Greek rationalism. They believe that the nonrational, story-oriented methods of the Old Testament and Jesus' parables are better than the careful definitions, categories and demonstrations of the Greeks. They believe that Greek rationalism is wholly a human vanity.

Such Christians are not to be laughed at. They are right to emphasize biblical warnings about the pride of the educated who forget that Jesus taught simple truths. They are right to warn that the devil can easily deceive and lead astray with false logic. But for all the dangers, God has given humans a talent that must be invested and increased. The road is dangerous; therefore, we must pray unceasingly for wisdom, humility and love. First and foremost: without love we are nothing.

But love is not just an interpersonal force. Love can be directed at institutions. Love can be directed at knowing. Love the university. Love the truth. Love and truth are bound up in the Creator of love and truth. When love infects your pursuit of truth and you pray for wisdom and humility, Greek rational tools cannot be used against you or against God. It was love of truth that founded the first universities.

Love God and do as you please. That was the dictum of one of the most important figures in the history of Christianity and the history of universities: St. Augustine. He wrote a book on methods of teaching and another book on the proper curriculum. He wrote often on logic and levels of certainty available to humans. Most importantly, he was convinced that our hearts will always be restless until they rest in God. Augustine lived about two hundred years after Origen and spent most of his life as a bishop in North Africa, preaching and advising and guiding a church. Augustine knew well the dangers of rationalism but recognized that God has given many of us the talent and the call to use it. More than any other early Christian leader, Augustine confirmed for the church the rightness of using Greek rationalism, especially lots of questioning, in the pursuit of God's truths. In the universities that the church would eventually build, Augustine towered, along with Plato and Aristotle, as a founder and model.

One of Augustine's most important books for the future development of universities was *On Christian Doctrine*. Contrary to its name, the book did not list doctrines that Christians were supposed to believe; rather, it dealt more with how Christians were to use rationalism in order to know what to believe. Augustine recommended the liberal arts curriculum used by Roman schools as a useful beginning for Christian education, especially mathematics because God seems to have created the universe with arithmetic and geometry in mind.

As for learning logic and history from pagan Greeks and Romans, Augustine advised Christians to take what is good and leave the rest. The Christian was to view the world at wide angles, asking new questions, finding truths not yet uncovered. Christians were not to burn pagan books or shun pagan ideas. Take the good. Find the true. If it was good or true, it was of God. Augustine did not make this up, but rather he was offering an educational application of Paul's advice to the Thessalonians: "Do not stifle inspiration or despise prophetic utterances, but test them all; keep hold of what is good and avoid all forms of evil" (1 Thess 5:19-22).

The Creation of Universities
Although Augustine had written about education and early Christians went to various types of schools or were tutored individually, there were no formal school systems before the Middle Ages, nor were there any specific institutions like modern universities where scholars gathered and students were awarded degrees. Such universities were first created over a thousand years after Christ's resurrection by Christians who wanted to educate Christians more systematically for the service of the increasingly complex church and state. Universities were job-oriented, just as they are today.

But the job training was not narrow. Universities were to produce thinkers, wise and knowledgeable men on whom responsibilities could be placed and from whom right decisions were expected. What God had revealed to humanity was the foundation of wisdom and knowledge, and the university helped build on that foundation. Teaching the right use of what God had given us was the university's goal. Rationality, rightly understood and rightly used, could not help but be useful to God and society.

Universities were first created in cities where scholars gathered. At first classes and living arrangements were very disorganized, but over the course of centuries sets of buildings were built and more unity imposed on the different disciplines of study. English and American universities were the first to emphasize parklike campuses in rural settings with students living on campus. Such campuses emphasized unified living and learning. Cities, however, have always been the greatest centers of higher education. Today most students are again commuters, living off campus as they did during the Middle Ages.

The feeling of unity breaks down in such a situation. Maybe this is for the best, since many students living on campuses seem to separate their university life from what they call *real* life in the *real* world. Maybe life has gotten too easy for young unmarried students living on campus, if they are not daily faced with integrating what they are learning with society at large. The university was never designed to be separated from real life, but rather it was to be at the core of reality where God's revelation and human knowledge met.

University Life and Real Life

One of the most influential students in history was Ignatius of Loyola. He was a commuter student at the University of Paris in the early sixteenth century. He had been a soldier, but after being wounded and leaving the army, he enrolled at the university and put his disciplined mind to work on the central question of reality: How can I best know, love and serve God? Loyola, along with a college friend and others, founded the Society of Jesus (the Jesuits), which became the most dynamic missionary order in the Roman Catholic Church—maybe in the history of the whole church. The many schools and colleges named after Loyola are tributes to an older commuter student who came to the university to learn about reality—not escape from reality.

The Jesuit colleges that still thrive throughout the world try to maintain the ideals of Loyola and the medieval university—the pursuit of the good and the true wherever they are found—because they know that everything that partakes of the good and the true is of God. The Jesuit professors who have been tortured and killed for their faith over the last four hundred years are Christian heroes. They carry on the tradition of Augustine: an intense love of truth that does not rest until it rests in God.

Disintegration and Secularization of Universities

Modern secular universities have reversed the process of integration advocated by Augustine in *On Christian Doctrine* and still practiced in Christian colleges. Disintegration is the tendency of the modern university. Integration—the process of integrating the good and true wherever it is found, the process advocated by Paul—has given way to a process of secularized disintegration. This secularization tries to split the human from the spiritual, with the hope of leaving the spiritual behind. Paul wrote, "Do not stifle inspiration" to Christians in order to keep their minds open, but now it is the modern university that must be told, "Do not stifle inspiration." Paul demanded that we "test" everything, especially the spiritual, but you will find that the secular university avoids rather than tests the spiritual.

However, the disintegration is not complete. It is in process, but it is ultimately impossible. There are too many faculty and students who understand that the honest pursuit of knowledge cannot begin with a decision *not* to test everything. They understand that the pursuit of truth cannot begin with a rule to avoid the spiritual. They still understand that the fundamental *uni* in *university* means the pursuit of a possible oneness and integration of truth, and they refuse to begin by assuming that there is no oneness and can be no integration.

I do not fear the modern tendency of splitting the spiritual from the curriculum. In order to support society universities must deal with morality, with the whole nature of humanity and with the possibility of purpose in the cosmos. Society pays for universities, and society demands an intelligent study of the spiritual along with study of the material. Remember the Indiana University Southeast mission statement!

The secularization of modern universities has been superficial. Public universities, of course, will never become Christian again in the narrow sense of being dominated by Christianity. They shouldn't if they want to serve our pluralistic society. Society in the Middle Ages was overwhelmingly Christian. It isn't today. But society and universities still pursue the good and the true. They want light. Christians have their place in universities, first because they are an important part of the society that pays for the institution, and second because the history of universities is Christian, and so we fit in well with traditional university values. Finally, we belong because we know some things about light and truth that need to be shared with the world.

Many big universities have a distinctive tower built in the middle of their campus. Those towers symbolize the unifying value of open-minded rationalism. They architecturally symbolize the hope in unified truth, an aspiration for a truth we Christians still believe is in God. The architect of Sather Tower at the University of California at Berkeley declared that his tower served to "point the University's way upward . . . unifying its ideals and punctuating its message." The architect, who was also a professor on campus, further declared of his tower: "Here is common ground, a common symbol, a common standard."

We Christians have a rightful place in the modern public university. When in doubt, look to the motto or mission statement of your school. Look to the towers and spires on campus. Know that our desire to pursue and integrate whatever is true and good, whether spiritual or secular, has a rightful place on campus.

— 6 —

Disunities
at the Modern
University

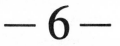

C hristians at a university have to learn to hate some aspects of the university while loving the core ideals. Christians are on the same team as many non-Christians in a contest to preserve universities from those who want to change them into competing financial units, into a collection of autonomous bastions of scientific orthodoxy and into institutions of social engineering. Maybe the worse foes in the contest are the students and faculty who have no concern for anything beyond self-gratification. The contest is against those who do not care about the mottoes and mission statements of universities. They are not concerned about encouraging the love of wisdom. They don't want to hear about the possibility of any truths that would stretch their world-view. They do not love the university.

I do not want to overdramatize this contest. I especially do not want to encourage you to be superficially judgmental of individual students and faculty. Let God pass judgment on individual souls and motives. God will separate the wheat from the weeds when it comes to people; our job is to separate the wheat from the weeds when it comes to what we hear in classrooms and read in books. Love and pray for your student and faculty neighbors. Pray for humility and wisdom. Look for the good, and you will find that the majority of faculty and students still pursue the true and the good wherever they can find it.

In this section on disunities, however, I have to be negative and point out the bad. A student needs to watch out for two types of disunity that are eating at the core of what universities are all about. The first is personal and affects the lives of students and professors; the second is institutional.

Personal Integrity and Academic Freedom

As for the first, modern students and faculty are systematically encouraged to divide their lives into boxes. Systematic training in graduate schools often teaches future professors to separate their religion and their consciences from their work as researchers and teachers. Religion becomes a hobby rather than a life-engulfing understanding. You will find that most of your faculty and fellow students do not oppose your Christianity; instead, they want you to treat your Christianity as merely a part of your life rather than the whole. They want you to disunite the life of your mind, to chop it up into mutually exclusive compartments. They are not antagonistic to the spiritual, they simply do not want rational spiritual beliefs to infringe on rational academic beliefs.

Aristotle, Origen, Augustine and Loyola would be horrified by the way many modern professors and students compartmentalize their lives. Even in areas not directly involving religion, professors are willing to teach things that no one is expected to live by. Professors are encouraged by the academic system to play games of speculation rather than pursue truth. Many books and articles are written in tiny little worlds of action and reaction that professors will confess to be absurd from the viewpoint of real life. I know too many authors who will cynically confess that their goal is simple publication, not a serious attempt to find life-engulfing truth.

To me the most striking examples of this disjunction between academic publication and life are played out on TV in Senate committee rooms. Often when professors are appointed to government positions they publicly disavow their published writings as mere "academic" speculations. In the 1980s several Supreme Court nominees carefully explained on TV that they did not really mean for society to live by what they wrote as law-school professors.

But some may say, "That's just politics," as if politics allows such sins. Let me offer another example of a similar disjunction between what is said "academically" and what is actually believed: an encounter between Albert Einstein, a Nobel Prize-winning physicist, and Thomas Hunt Morgan, a Nobel Prize-winning geneticist. Morgan was on the faculty of the California Institute of Technology (Caltech) during a sunny winter when the university paid Einstein to come for a visit. Upon meeting the geneticist, Einstein asked Morgan, one Nobel Prize winner to another, "Do you think you will ever be able to explain in terms of chemistry or physics so important a biological phenomenon as first love?"

Morgan later recounted his answer: "I tried to explain something about the connection between sense organs and the brain and hormones." When Morgan was then asked if he really believed what he told Einstein, he said, "No, but I had to say something to him."

This is a superficial example, but it sheds light on what happens every day in classrooms across the country. A disjunction of life and academic thought is helping to destroy the unity that was the *uni* in *university.* Einstein, like any inquisitive student, asks one of the *big* questions: Can biology explain love? The professor, feeling obligated to be the prize-winning biologist rather than the commonsensical human, gives an answer that he does not believe. This is a disunity. Professors and overly zealous students often feel obligated to defend the absurd or narrow ideas and implications of a single discipline as if they were defense lawyers, when the ideals of the university call for open minds and frank discussion.

If I may offer a plug for Christian colleges at this point: In those colleges integration of thought and life is still expected and is a major force of unification. Robert Gundry, a professor of New Testament at Westmont College in Santa Barbara, got himself into a lot of trouble because his research affected his beliefs in a way that seemed to threaten the ideals of the community that financially supports the college. At Christian colleges people hold professors accountable for what they write, think and teach. At Westmont, controversy ensued. Gundry refused to renounce his book. Financial backers in Los Angeles called for his dismissal. Westmont decided to support the professor at the risk of losing some funding. Though many tensions continue, the cause of truth was served in sincere debate, with no one claiming academic immunity to write what they did not believe or say what they did not mean.

The controversy at Westmont began in the early 1980s. At the end of the decade a national debate developed over the similar struggles of Charles Curran, a professor of moral theology at Catholic University in Washington, D.C. Curran wrote a book and taught in class a position on birth control which is not the doctrine of the Roman Catholic Church. The papacy asked that Curran be barred from teaching moral theology classes. Curran was willing to compromise but demanded the right to teach the results of his research. Controversy ensued, and Curran eventually moved to another Roman Catholic university, one less under the influence of the papacy. Whether one agrees with Curran or not, a professor's firm commitment to the results of research is an honorable thing. The fact that controversy developed is also good. The cause of truth is served when a society and its university professors engage in sincere debate with no one claiming the separation of real life from academic thought.

Such is the creative interaction of conscientious faculty, their colleges and the societies that support them. It happens at small Christian colleges but is increasingly rare at large secular universities. The January 19, 1994, edition of the *Chronicle of Higher Education* reports a situation where a professor is trying to teach his ideas but is being suppressed by his colleagues, who want him to split his life and thought into boxes. After years of teaching evolution, Dean Kenyon, a biologist at San Francisco State University, now thinks that the evidence seems to point to "an intelligent agent" responsible for creating life on earth. Kenyon's colleagues are trying to force him to teach a more purely Darwinian form of evolutionary theory. Kenyon, to his credit, will not split his life and teaching into separate boxes.

The pursuit of truth lives when scholars like Kenyon integrate their life and thought and stand firmly on the result. Open debate, especially among colleagues on an issue within their expertise, is always a sign of health. Many secular universities are losing this type of healthy debate because scholars, unlike Kenyon, are willing to teach a dogmatic orthodoxy even if they think otherwise. Peer pressure among the faculty is becoming more important than freedom of thought. It is peer review that usually controls salary increases and promotions. Some think a raise and promotion is worth the price of academic freedom.

I should point out that I am making a generalization about the disunity of life and thought that I perceive to be increasingly prevalent. On the other hand, I know that most of my colleagues in secular universities try to live up to the ideals of the university mottoes and mission statements. Across the nation, however, there is an academic trend toward disintegration rather than integration.

Having outlined the problem of personal disintegration in universities, I now turn to the second, more institutional disintegration: radical skepticism.

Radical Skepticism

Radical skepticism is antagonistic to the ideals of universities and must be distinguished from healthy forms of skepticism. René Descartes, who is famous for doubting everything, was a healthy skeptic. He used skepticism to break down encrusted ideas in order to build newer and stronger foundations for newer and more accurate understandings. Doubt is an important academic tool. We analyze by pulling something apart so that we can then assemble better understanding. Healthy skepticism has a positive goal. Radical skepticism has no positive goal and is essentially the systematic avoidance of any firm knowledge and understanding.

Radical skepticism is basically malicious because it has no positive or productive goal. It strives for the bliss of ignorance by finding a "con" to balance every "pro." Radical skeptics insist that the only absolute truth is that there is no absolute truth. They want to destroy the positive pursuit of truth by loving paradoxes, conundrums and the weaknesses of the human mind. They *want* to not know. They *want* the bliss of ignorance.

Such skepticism is not wholly malicious. It is important for wise people to recognize that there are some truths in it. The book of Ecclesiastes in the Old Testament advises small, frail human beings to adopt some of the perspectives of radical skepticism. But radical skepticism is not the whole of truth. Ecclesiastes alone leads nowhere. Plato, Aristotle, Augustine, Aquinas, Descartes, Locke and the most productive thinkers in Western civilization have fought against the destructive effects of radical skepticism. Universities were founded, in part, to counteract radical skepticism. They are intended to be productive, not destructive. Universities *want* knowledge. Traditional universities emphasize the constructive powers of logic, mathematics, geometry and natural science. They are centers of integrating information toward new and greater understanding and of educating new generations of thinkers capable of even newer and greater levels of understanding.

Modern public universities are still for the most part productive, but the influence of radical skepticism and its destructive form of negativity is increasing. There is a growing cynicism about the possibility of the productive use of human reason. Some disciplines, such as the study of literature, seem increasingly bent on destroying themselves, seduced by the lure of radical skepticism.

Radical skepticism insists that humans actually do not know anything and that our rationality is a mirage. Augustine and Descartes pointed out that humans do know some things. That a human knows he or she exists is a starter. Universities since the Middle Ages have emphasized what humans *do* know. Humans *know* that colors are not shapes. They *know* that "Danger: 10,000 volts" means "Don't touch." Radical skeptics can play intellectual games to attack all knowledge, but our lives and the history of universities testify to the error of radical skepticism.

Skeptics should always be welcome in good universities. The debates they encourage are healthy. However, radical skepticism is a rational game by people who think that being rational is meaningless. Radical skepticism is not for the wise. Some people think that negativity and cynicism are signs of wisdom. University professors and students are famous in novels and movies for mistaking cynicism and negativity for wisdom. You will encounter professors and students enthralled by the implications of radical skepticism. Realize though that they cannot truly live a life of radical skepticism. Realize also that the university needs to be reminded of the frailties of human reason so that it can reach even higher levels of understanding. Just as the Bible includes the book of Ecclesiastes without expecting us to be so seduced by that book that we forget the rest of the Bible, so too your education should include some radical skepticism without allowing it to seduce you into its all-embracing, destructive swirl. If radical skepticism continues to increase at universities, we can expect universities to disintegrate and eventually become worthless to society.

So the modern university is a field of contest between those who hold to its mottoes and mission statements and those who abandon them by either separating academics from life or embracing radical skepticism. What is the Christian student to do? Seek out other students and faculty who hold tightly to the traditional values of a university. Join forces with those who vigorously pursue understanding with open minds and desire to integrate their lives with their thinking.

There is an old model of the institutional church as containing within it a hidden church of true believers. If we adapt Jesus' parable of the wheat and the weeds, we can picture the wheat of the hidden church growing side by side with the weeds within the institution until Jesus culls the wheat at the judgment. The image could also be applied to a university. The Christian at a modern university can register and pay tuition to the whole institution while consciously joining the hidden university within made up of the professors and students who seek truths to live by. Remember that in a diversified secular university the hidden university is not made up of just Christians or members of your particular form of Christianity. There will be many from different religions, philosophies and theologies who share the hope in unity that originally empowered universities. Love them as neighbors and team-mates who share the desire to know the truth that will set them free.

—7—

The Progress
of Knowledge

Truth, wrote Francis Bacon, is the "daughter of time." Bacon was a Christian philosopher who believed that truth was alive in God. Throughout our history most Christians have believed that time has a beginning in creation, that Christ was the fullness of time and that Christ will come back at the end of time. We believe that time is one of God's creations and that it is moving somewhere. God has a plan for time. All things eventually work together for good for God's children. Time is the successive revelation of God's will, and God uses time to gradually teach and guide humanity. In our Christian understanding of time, God's truths are not passive. They are active. Truth is the daughter of time, because God's truths pursue us more than we pursue truths. Even though Christians may think wrong things for ages, and our finite minds will always mix error and truth, the Holy Spirit is active, gradually teaching humanity more truth.

Some Christians believe in a golden age of knowledge in the past. They believe that ever since the Garden of Eden, or maybe apostolic times, humanity has been losing knowledge and moving away from God's truth. Though possibly this is valid in some respects, most Christians have believed that the Holy Spirit has continued to help us accumulate and build more knowledge. Let me offer two examples I think we can all agree on.

Two Examples

Our modern view of Christian marriage is not in the Old Testament and is only hinted at in the New. Modern Christian marriage, founded on the free choice of two people filled with love and celebrated in church as a covenant with God, is a relatively new idea. Marriages among the early Greeks, Hebrews and Romans were primarily economic and political arrangements. Our modern understanding of marriage has some foundations in the New Testament but is not clearly defined there. Probably the most important statement about marriage in the New Testament is the image of the church as the bride of Christ.

The early medieval church began to develop the implications of marriage as a spiritual union similar to that of Christ and the church. Church lawyers and theologians began to define and regulate marriage and family relations to conform to this image and other New Testament passages. Later medieval theologians decided that marriage could be considered a holy sacrament like baptism. In subsequent centuries the Holy Spirit guided the church toward our modern understanding of marriage as a sacred commitment and fundamental spiritual unit with special privileges and responsibilities. Whether marriage ranks as a sacrament is debated among churches, but the idea of marriage as a freely covenanted spiritual union is the generally accepted view, one that has been developed over the past two thousand years. Problems such as divorce policies and the responsibilities of each marriage partner beset modern marriage, but I know of no one who wishes to return to the marriage practices of biblical times.

The purpose and practice of marriage have changed through time because the Holy Spirit has been teaching and guiding us. I praise God for the bond of love in my family and for the cultural developments in history that allow my family to exist as it does. I have hope that the Holy Spirit will teach us more about marriage and families in the future. What once was only seen through a glass darkly is becoming more clear.

A much more mundane example of the progress of knowledge is the development of credit and interest-bearing loans. As for general economic policies, I believe the Bible has much to teach us; however, if you look for the term *usury* in a concordance you will find a number of passages listed that condemn the practice of charging interest on a loan. Practical necessity in the Middle Ages and the modern thinking of academic economists have taught us a new way of interpreting the Bible on the subject. We now interpret the biblical condemnations as condemnations against charging inappropriate usury rather than usury itself.

As in the case of marriage, it took centuries to come to this interpretation. The Greeks, Hebrews, Romans and early Christians did not develop a system of lending money on interest, and the "money-lender" was painted as an extortioner. But money lending is important to people trying to buy farms, start a business or buy a car. Why shouldn't a money-lending bank earn a profit from a person's use of the bank's money? I know of no modern Christians who consider banks to be evil for lending money while charging appropriate interest. Most of us could never afford a house or buy a reliable car, let alone afford college, if the modern system of credit did not exist.

Both of these examples give an indication of how knowledge has progressed. We have not universally progressed. We are not better or wiser people than those who lived in the past. We have also lost some of the knowledge that existed in the past. We are, however, the beneficiaries of long progress in some areas of knowledge. The Holy Spirit has been active, and universities have been important participants in the progressive revelation of knowledge. Universities were created and thrived because most Christians believed in the progress of knowledge through time. University Christians believed that God was working with them and that as they pursued knowledge, the Holy Spirit would help them learn things never before known.

Progress Rightly Understood

But the pursuit and progress of knowledge can be misused and misdirected. Better technologies of evil can be developed, better means of oppression, better justifications for genocide or life-boat ethics. Certainly university Christians have never advocated mere curiosity or indulging in intellectual promiscuity. The tools of logic are sacred tools to be used in concert with prayer and proper reverence for what God has already revealed. Mere curiosity and narrow logic can be tools of the devil. Intellectual promiscuity is like sexual promiscuity: the taking of what is good and holy and ruining it. With prayer and grace from the Holy Spirit, however, the university can be a place where scholars accumulate and increase humanity's storehouse of truths.

The modern public university, for all its disunities, still has a belief in the progress of knowledge. Fundamentally, university professors believe in the ordered accumulation and progress of knowledge. The main duty of the campus library is to store and disseminate accumulating knowledge. Ralph Waldo Emerson wrote that all professors are really only librarians. To a certain extent it is true. But professors and students also pursue new information. The university is a place in pursuit of knowledge in the hope of increasing knowledge. To believe in the possibility that knowledge increases is to believe in a fundamental order and truth. Truth is the daughter of time. We now see through a glass darkly, but someday we will see face to face. If we continue to pursue truth, I believe God will help guide us. As long as universities proclaim the ideals of light and truth, God will bless them.

The modern secular university, however, is rife with mere curiosity and intellectual promiscuity. The progress it believes in is much influenced by an anti-Christian philosophy called positivism. This philosophy was founded by Auguste Comte, a Frenchman who died in 1857. Comte is also considered the founder of the discipline of sociology. Comte synthesized a way of thinking about progress that greatly influenced the development of modern public universities. He believed that there were essentially three stages to the progress of knowledge. The first stage is religious and primitive. This is the stage we Christians are stuck in. The second stage is metaphysical. This stage still believes in the spiritual and is God-oriented, but it is no longer tied to any specific religion or sacred text such as the Bible. The third and final stage of progress, the stage that Comte and many university professors think they are part of, is the stage of relativism. When people have advanced beyond their primitive beliefs, they come to "realize" that there is no absolute truth, no sacred text and no authority outside of themselves, and that the ignorant masses are subject to social "forces."

Positivism is falling apart at universities. It is too simplistic. Not only does it denigrate religion and the foundations of morality, it also assumes too much about the cosmos and the ability of humans to understand the cosmos. It is also too triumphalistic. My perception is that university faculties now are more humble than the university faculties of the early twentieth century. I take this as progress.

Part II

Christians in the Classroom

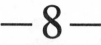

— 8 —

Being Aware
of Limits
& Strategies

Raise your hand. Ask questions. Be prepared. Read all of the assignment. Do your homework. Don't be intimidated. Let the teacher and the rest of the class know you are interested. Other students will follow you. You can be the spark that transforms a boring class into an exciting class. A university classroom can be one of the most wonderful places on earth when the students and teachers are working together. It can just as easily be one of the most terrible. Do your part to make it wonderful.

Up until now, this book has dealt with generalities, and I have written about the physical and intellectual environment that makes a university. The rest of the book will be more specific and practical, and I will discuss what actually happens in classrooms. I am not going to present any actual class material but rather give insights into the deep strategies and limits infused in lectures and textbooks. I hope it helps you ask better questions in order to learn more from your classes, and that it gives you a Christian perspective on the basic strategies of academic study. This perspective can help you ask intelligent questions and understand the answers given in class.

Before we move into the strategies used in your classes, I want to digress into some practical advice: Do not use the material presented in this chapter to attack non-Christian professors. I have seen Christians attack their professors, and in fact I have been attacked for not adhering to someone else's orthodoxy. Nothing productive comes from such attacks.

Antagonistic Questioning

When I was an undergraduate, I was in a religious studies class called "From Augustine to Luther" where a few Christians would regularly attack the professor and disrupt the class. One time the professor, who I grant was overly pleased with himself, acted out the conversation between God and Satan from the book of Job with embellishments to make us all laugh. He did this in the context of explaining Augustine's views on the problem of evil—a subject that can be boring. The clutch of antagonistic students immediately raised their hands and began pointing out the little errors in the teacher's skit. I remember vividly how they all held their Bibles open to the book of Job. I got mad at them.

Throughout the course, they dragged their perspective of biblical infallibility into almost every subject we discussed, so that the professor's lectures lost their continuity and he became so flustered that he obviously hated being in the room. I grant that the professor did not show much respect for the Bible, and he was one of those types who direct most of their attention to the best-looking women in the class; however, his portrayal of God and Satan was not blasphemous. He was trying to make his point in an interesting way. The antagonistic students served only to disrupt the class so that learning became harder for everyone.

Always allow the professor to stick to the subject of the lecture.

The professor must control the overall direction of the class, because he or she is responsible to the university and the other students in the class.

In the classroom I want open and productive debate. I am employed by the state to help students think rationally and communicate their ideas orally and in writing. I am paid to educate liberally—to encourage free thinking and open debate; however, free-flowing debate is different from antagonism and disruption. Disruption by any person or group for political, religious or personal reasons has to be suppressed when it is unproductive. I have been interrupted during lectures by political ideologues of the left and of the right, homosexuals and antihomosexuals, prochoice and prolife advocates, and various Christians and anti-Christians with axes to grind. I often run into rabid anti-Catholics and antifundamentalists in my classes; these students usually are irrationally antagonistic because of some perceived injustice done to them when they were children.

I try to turn such interruptions into productive debate. If the students refuse to be open-minded or charitable, I cut the students off and move on. It's my job. I must maintain control of the overall direction of the class.

Antagonistic questions are seldom productive. Productive debate requires listening and willingness to understand other perspectives; unproductive debate is rooted in a simple desire for conquest at any cost.

Raise your hand in class. Ask questions about how what is being taught relates to Christianity. Christianity, along with other religions, is a dominant factor in the American culture that supports universities. Religion is never an inappropriate subject for class discussion. Your professor is employed to guide such discussions and should encourage students to relate classroom knowledge to public life. But ask questions in love and with a true desire to understand. Feel free to disagree, but let the professor run the classroom. Pursue your questions after class. Maybe buy your professor a cup of coffee after class so that you can have some time to get to know each other.

As a sophomore fulfilling general education requirements, I took a film studies course that the professor designed around existentialism in 1960s artistic movies. I would often ask questions in class, and several times he cut me off. I deserved it. I did not want to talk about the camera angles used to express ideas, I wanted to talk about existentialism—a loose and generally antireligious view of life. I was becoming an obstruction in the flow of the course, so instead of yelling at me, he invited me to talk to him after class. In his office we had a good discussion with no reference to films. We also ended up cutting a deal: I would read a book he recommended to me (*Zen and the Art of Motorcycle Maintenance*), and he would read a book I recommended to him (*The Abolition of Man* by C. S. Lewis).

Looking back, I realize that I learned a lot about the meanings behind camera angles and lighting in his class and also enjoyed reading the book he recommended. He certainly hated Christianity, but he succeeded in offering a good course where I learned much. He was a good teacher. So was the teacher in my "Augustine to Luther" class. For all its problems, I look back on that class as one of the most influential classes in my college life. We spent three weeks reading and discussing Augustine. I don't remember much the professor said, but I was introduced to one of the most inspiring thinkers in history.

Let the professor design and run the class. Professors usually know what they are doing.

The Limits of University Logic

Being logical is the goal of almost every class in a university. Logic is what you are usually actually being taught, no matter what your course is titled, no matter whether your professor wears a lab coat or tweed coat. Logic is a set of strategies for being reasonable, rational and scholarly. Logic is a toolbox of strategies. Some tools are better than others for specific jobs. The choice of tool limits what can be done. A wrench serves wrench work, but choosing a wrench means that one can't tighten a screw or saw a board without changing tools. Being logical is the ability to know the strengths and weaknesses of the different tools and strategies available. Being logical means understanding that logic is merely a set of tools, not an end in itself.

The tools of logic can be very specialized—such as the rules disciplines have for creating terms and definitions—or very general. The most general tool of logic upon which the university is constructed is the model of geometry. In geometry, using axioms and little bits of knowledge derived from axioms, a person demonstrates something. Taking what is demonstrated, one then gathers more little bits of knowledge to demonstrate something larger. Then that large something is gathered together with other things to demonstrate even larger things. The process yields a structure that looks like an inverted pyramid. Individual stones of knowledge, pieced together, yield a massive structure of knowledge that is continually expanding. Even when someone's demonstration destroys some other scholar's demonstration, the hope is that the removal of a weak stone will make the whole structure stronger.

Universities are optimistic. They are geometrical. They work toward the future to create something bigger. Their goal is the continual expansion of knowledge built upon a multitude of logical demonstrations rooted in some initial assumptions. Christians make excellent academics. We have a religion that emphasizes the order and unity of knowledge in a way that supports the optimism of geometrical logic.

Axioms: Initial Assumptions

Although Christians share with secular academics the use of the geometric model of logic, there is a difficulty. The logical base—the axioms, the initial assumptions, sometimes called "first principles"— used at secular universities are smaller in number than the set used by Christian academics. Christians in secular universities must work back and forth between the smaller and the larger set of axioms.

Let's look more carefully at axioms. The deepest debates in all universities are about axioms, because not only are they the foundation on which all geometrical logic is built, they are also the spiritual or metaphysical part of human knowledge. Axioms are the unavoidable spiritual commitment of all university professors and rational people.

I may be using the term *spiritual* too loosely, but let me explain. To me axioms are spiritual because they come from a person's intuition or common sense. Rational people have to rely on something deep within them. They have to submit to initial assumptions derived from something they do not fully understand. Even if a person's intuition and common sense push him or her to say that there is no spiritual world, only a material universe, that person is still using something that cannot be materially explained: intuition and what he or she perceives to be common sense.

I am not insistent about the terms used. The point I want to make is that the underlying assumptions or axioms of all university disciplines are very slippery. Even if one insists that they are not spiritual, they have the slipperiness of assumed universality.

Christians generally are comfortable with the idea of axioms. We believe that they are the fundamental building blocks of knowledge and that God implanted them in our minds. We are comfortable with the idea that God gives most humans a conscience that knows some fundamental rights and wrongs and has some basic ideas as to who our Creator is. But for academics who do not want to speculate about divine sources of knowledge, axioms are uncomfortable.

Most professors avoid talking about axioms in the classroom. Axioms complicate already complicated issues. For example, one of Euclid's geometrical axioms states, "A whole is greater than its parts." This is an axiom because it is unprovable. It seems absolutely obvious. That is the point. It is an axiom because it seems obvious but cannot be proven. Euclid accepted it as true and then built on it. All of us who have taken high-school geometry just have to accept it and work on top of it. Why couldn't Euclid prove it? I am not sure I know well enough to explain it. Like most people, I just accept it and move on.

An axiom in geometry or logic is something that cannot be demonstrated but we accept as true. In the Declaration of Independence the "self-evident truths" are the axioms upon which American ideals are constructed. We cannot prove that you and I have the right to life, liberty and the pursuit of happiness, but we accept that it is true. We cannot prove that all humans are created equal. We cannot prove these things so we just declare them obvious or "self-evident." Axioms are self-evident truths. We know them internally, and they cannot be demonstrated externally to someone else in the way that the answer to a math problem or the conclusion of a history paper can be demonstrated. We know axioms by intuition. The fundamental truth in university logic is that all our human knowledge is ultimately founded on personal intuition.

Intuition

Aristotle, the father of Greek logic, knew the importance of intuition. In the conclusion of his *Posterior Analytics,* one of the founding books of logic, he declared that the two strongest types of human knowledge are intuition and the conclusions of logical demonstrations. He went on to say that, because logical demonstrations are built on intuition, intuition is the higher and more important of the two types of knowledge. Intuition, he wrote, is the "originative source" of knowledge.

What is intuition? It is that spiritual part of us on the borderlands with the divine. It is where humans who are blessed with properly functioning minds grasp an array of truths about the cosmos and our own existence. Intuitions must be tested, since there are false intuitions; however, if we confidently know something in our heart that is as obvious and self-evident to us as that all humans have a right to life, liberty and the pursuit of happiness, then we have grasped a true intuition. We Christians believe that, by grace, God gives some humans a true intuition of the truth of Christianity. By grace, Christians have intuition of some truths that are not in the intuition of non-Christians. This is one of the reasons there are different sets of axioms that create differences between Christian logic and university logic.

University logic purposefully tries to use as few axioms as possible and wants to discourage the use of religious intuitions. The reason modern secular universities try to limit the use of self-evident bits of knowledge is that they believe that the fewer the number of axioms, the larger the number of people who will be able to agree with the conclusion. This is probably true; however, when academics limit the number of axioms, they also limit their conclusions and confine the growth of knowledge within more limited boundaries than Christian logicians.

Limited—this is the fundamental character of public universities. The great myth of modern science and modern universities is that they have *unlimited* possibilities. This is false. By limiting the use of what humans know internally as axioms, they greatly limit the successful use of logic. It is a simple formula of logic: limit the sources of knowledge and you limit the range of conclusions. God, by grace working internally, has convinced Christians of many truths that we are normally not allowed to use in academic demonstrations at secular universities. That God has a purpose for us is just as unprovable as the geometrical axiom "The whole is greater than its parts"; however, universities disallow the use of the Christian axiom but allow the geometrical. The biggest difference between premodern and modern universities (or Christian and secular universities) is that modern universities avoid or normally disallow axioms based in religion. For example, universities used to accept as axioms the existence of human souls and of consciences, but such religious axioms are now usually avoided. The tools for studying the mind and soul that universities used to use have been put back into the toolbox and replaced by different tools better able to study the brain's relationship to behavior. The new tools are good, but they limit what can be done.

What You Start with Affects What You End Up With

When the modern university avoids the use of spiritual axioms, it steers the direction of accumulating knowledge in nonspiritual directions. How can the university research and develop more knowledge about the spiritual aspects of the cosmos or about God's ways of communicating with humans when it does not allow the fundamental premise of a spiritual realm or existence of a communicating God?

What you start with affects what you end up with.

For example: non-Euclidean geometries were developed in the nineteenth century by experimentally limiting the number of axioms. Given Euclid's ten axioms, the normal geometry you learned in high school follows logically. In the nineteenth century, some geometers decided to use only nine of the ten. They abandoned the one about parallel lines never meeting. This completely changed the logical course of their geometry and led to new alternative geometries studied in college. The radical differences between Euclidean and non-Euclidean geometries exemplifies the importance of choosing which axioms to use. Changing from ten to nine axioms created a whole new set of courses in modern universities. A whole academic field within math departments was created by the deletion of one small assumption. *What you start with affects what you end up with.*

Shrink or expand the number of axioms used in any study and you change both what you can study and the type of conclusions you are able to achieve. The difference between premodern and modern psychology is one of the clearest examples of this. The modern psychology you learn today is very different from premodern psychology because it does not allow axioms dealing with spiritual matters and it accepts an axiom from Darwinian science. The result: modern psychology is good at things that premodern psychology was not good at, and premodern psychology was good at things that modern psychology is not good at.

Psychology: A Gain Here Is a Loss There

Psychology began as the study of the human soul and was originally taught in universities as part of philosophy. The three main methods of studying the human soul were (1) introspectively analyzing one's own mind, especially listening to what the Holy Spirit communicates to humans internally, (2) reading and thinking about what the Bible teaches, especially the implications of being created in the image of God and yet fallen and finite, and (3) observing other people and comparing accounts of their minds with one's own mind. Psychology in the seventeenth and eighteenth centuries was a branch of what some called *pneumatology*, the study of spiritual beings—that is, God, angels, demons and humans. It was all very scientific and rational. Logic, the toolbox, had many good tools for this study. Aristotle himself had written on the soul.

Great advances were made in the old psychology. People were able to map what they called the *faculties* of the soul, which were described as being woven together in complex ways that affected each person's understanding of God, self and society. The crisis that occurred when the Protestant churches broke from the Roman Catholic Church caused great university professors such as Philipp Melanchthon to write psychology/philosophy textbooks that advanced our understanding of the human conscience and helped society become more tolerant of religious diversity. Later in the eighteenth century, professors of moral philosophy continued to research and teach important advances in psychology that could have led to a much better understanding of our souls today. But modern psychology began in the nineteenth century with different goals and a smaller set of axioms.

Instead of the soul, modern psychology (along with other modern disciplines) is interested in behavior and how the brain is connected to behavior. Instead of the conscience, modern psychology is interested in the mechanics of perception, the way some behaviors can be conditioned and the functioning of memory, hormones and genes in determining human behavior. The old psychology of introspection into the God-designed faculties of our spiritual selves disappeared from the academic curriculum of most universities. The goals changed. The logical strategies changed. The tools changed. Therefore the conclusions changed.

Raise your hand in your introductory psych class and ask about possible spiritual qualities of human beings. The professor will explain what modern psychology does and does not do. Your professor will explain that the logical strategy of modern psychology, along with that of neuroscience, neuropsychology, psychobiology and other related, specialized academic fields, normally rules out God, even though God may exist. The strategy has limited the axioms in a way that has led to great productivity in some areas of knowledge, such as drug treatments for depression or behavioral disorders.

Your professor will probably also be able to point out that this productivity in one area has limited productivity in another. In psychology, increasing understanding of God's interaction with our souls has stopped. The field, as studied at secular universities, no longer advances our understanding of the conscience or the soul. The tools and strategies adopted today have their upside and their downside. A gain here is a loss there.

A Modern Axiom: Animal Minds = Human Minds

The history of psychology exemplifies the fact that when decisions are made to limit the type of axioms allowed in universities, the type of conclusions are also limited. Modern university disciplines are not unlimited. Modern academics have chosen a path that helps them be productive in some things but nonproductive in others. As a university student, feel free to raise questions about the axioms being used in the class. Ask about the possible spiritual axioms that have been ruled out. Engage in discussions that help everyone understand the limitations of all sciences. Christians do not necessarily have a better logical strategy than non-Christians. All strategies are finite and have their pluses and minuses, their ups and downs.

The disciplines today that study the brain and behavior often seem to teach non-Christian conclusions. Don't be antagonistic, but do ask questions. Always keep in mind that sometimes the conclusions being taught are the simple result of the fact that no spiritual axioms are being used.

Charles Darwin, the nineteenth-century proponent of biological evolution, helped change the scientific study of the brain and behavior when he wrote that "there is no fundamental difference between man and the higher mammals in the mental faculties." Modern scientists adopted Darwin's idea as axiomatic and started studying human brains and behavior by experimenting on animal brains. After accepting such an axiom, scientists have been able to discover chemical variations in animal brains that also affect human brains. Modern science, using drugs developed on animals, can help people suffering from depression or hyperactivity have more stable lives. This is a good development that results from a logical strategy based on an axiom that animal and human minds are essentially the same.

However, Darwin's idea that there is *no fundamental difference* is an assumption that we Christians cannot fully accept. You might have a psychology or biology professor say something in class that gives the impression that science has proven that humans are just animals and that even our love, joy and other human traits are nothing more than extensions of animal traits. If your professor seems to teach this, you should ask questions. The professor is probably not saying what you think you hear. Such things are impossible to prove by the strategies they are using. Ask for more information, and the professor will probably be more careful to explain that what science has proven is very different from a conjecture about human love or joy.

For example, the October 1993 issue of *Nature,* a major scientific magazine, carried an article about family love in animals. A group of scientists from the Laboratory of Neurophysiology at the National Institute of Mental Health reported on experiments dealing with the influence of some neuropeptides (hormones) on the family life of little rodents called voles. Voles were studied because they mate monogamously and male voles show parental "affiliation" to young voles by keeping them warm and grooming them. The scientists found that the family activities of most of the male voles they studied were affected by the concentration of a neuropeptide in their brains. The article was about voles, but because of the Darwinian axiom that human brains are like animal brains, the article points toward the possibility of similar situations in human brains. The scientists, however, had only proven something about a rodent. They ended their article with the warning "The extent to which any single peptide subserves any aspect of social bonding in humans remains entirely speculative."

Even though the scientists made this warning, the study was reported nationally in newspapers as a breakthrough in understanding family love in humans. Many professors who teach introductory courses in behavioral sciences will probably never read the article in *Nature* but will have read the newspaper version, and they will report to their classes that "studies show that parental love of children may be caused by hormones." There is nothing wrong in this. Introductory courses have to be loose and broad. The professor has said "may be caused." He or she has not said "is." However, the class may get the impression that family love in humans is actually being "explained" by neurophysiology as an animal behavior controlled by chemicals.

Watch out! If you hear something like this that seems so antagonistic to both Christianity and common sense, then raise your hand and ask the professor to explain the situation more fully. A good professor will explain that the leap from male voles huddling with baby voles to dads tucking their children in at night is beyond the limitations of modern academic science.

We who teach at universities know that our knowledge is very limited and our logic frail. There is a great cartoon that shows a scientist writing a formula on a chalkboard. The left and right sides of the chalkboard are filled with equations, but in the middle of the formula is written "(a miracle happens here)." The truth is that this cartoon describes almost everything you will learn at the university.

Careful Listening and Deep Questioning

Understand that teachers in classrooms are often not very precise in their language. Teachers are trying to inspire a class and make the subject as exciting as possible. Professors indulge in rhetoric, the artful organization of speech. Sometimes this can backfire and students hear the opposite of what the professor wanted them to hear.

Let me take the academic study of parental love a little further to illustrate the importance of listening carefully and weighing what a professor says. Steven Pinker, director of the Center for Cognitive Neuroscience at Massachusetts Institute of Technology, wrote a review in *The New York Times* which has all the marks of a good lecture.

It starts with a gripping statement: "The mind is a product of the brain, and the brain is a product of evolution's organizing force, natural selection. This simple Darwinian truth has illuminated vast stretches of our mental life."

Wow! The authority of such a statement! The way he says "simple Darwinian truth" implies that anyone who might disagree has Jell-O for a brain. (His statement is actually a very dubious axiom, not necessarily a "truth.")

Pinker goes on to talk with the same authority about a new book on "evolutionary biology":

> Take parenting. . . . [The author] explains how it arises from selfish genes: any gene that shapes an animal to help its relatives will, with some probability, be favoring copies of that gene sitting inside those relatives. Thus . . . parents are predicted to nurture each offspring in proportion to the offspring's actuarially estimated reproductive potential.

There, couched in professorial language, is a ruthlessly powerful swipe at something that almost all of us hold dear and know deeply in our being. Parental love is reduced to species perpetuation—or "actuarially estimated reproductive potential."

But the good professor has a kicker. He has grabbed us with an opening line. He has lectured about a theory without giving any alternatives. Then, in the last five minutes of a class session, when the lazy students are folding their notebooks and capping their pens, the teacher opens up a whole new way of seeing everything he has just said. In the conclusion Pinker says the theory he has been presenting is oversimplified. In the last minute of our imaginary class, Pinker goes so far as to open the door for a Christian interpretation of the material: "An evolutionary psychology that sees the moral sense as a biological adaptation is perfectly compatible with an ethical philosophy that sees moral principles as having a logic and justification of their own."

Wow again! Pinker has not defended Christianity. He doesn't seem to have any interest in the truth of Christianity. But, as a good professor, he has opened up a variety of options for his listener/readers to think about, after he has first presented a powerful set of ideas. If he was giving the lecture to me, I would raise my hand or head up to his lectern after class. Here is a man who knows much while seeing weaknesses, strengths and possible areas of synthesis in a crucially important subject of human life and university study. I can learn from a man like this.

The trouble is found in the lazy students who didn't listen carefully at the end of the lecture. They went away thinking Pinker was clearly teaching that parental love is just an evolutionary adaption. Don't believe everything you hear in class, because what you hear might not have been what was said.

Students must listen carefully, and sometimes they must fill in the blanks and read between the lines. Almost everything a professor says in an undergraduate class can be prefaced by hedgings and warnings. The psychologist who says in class that parental love may be caused by hormones or evolution is not too different from me when I say in my classes that Alexander Hamilton probably had no selfish intent when he proposed the financing system of George Washington's administration. The psychologist could spend precious time explaining the reasons for saying "may be" instead of "is," just as I could spend time defining "selfish" and why I said "probably," but teachers want to keep classes moving because students are easily bored.

Most teachers, though, are happy to stop for a question. Professors have usually given the lecture a hundred times. Any question is new and unique. It is the questions that make education personal and justify the cost of having a living professor rather than a TV screen. It is the questions that make classroom lectures fun. The psychology professors I know would happily stop to talk about the implications of an animal experiment for something so complex as human love.

The worst thing that happens in universities is that students easily start thinking from impressions drawn from a class rather than from what was actually said in a class. Too many students want things black and white rather than gray. They forget that the psychologist said "may be" and I said "probably." They start putting away their notebooks and capping their pens when professors are summing up the lecture. Most professors are at their best in the last five minutes of class. Be careful. Ask questions. Listen. If a statement made in class is important to you, then follow it up—ask the professor what exactly he or she meant, ask what books or experiments demonstrated it, go to the library and read about the subject.

Textbooks

A word on textbooks: Most textbooks are *Reader's Digest* versions of scholarship. Blatant fact: Textbooks oversimplify things so much that they often distort the truth. (I have oversimplified some things in this book in order to keep it simple and moving.) If something in a textbook (or this book) interests you, then go find out more information. If something you learn in a textbook indicates that you should change your thinking on an important subject—wait. Research further. Ask your professor for the whole story, read the related books in the bibliography, ask other students and faculty what they think. Talk to educated people you respect.

Finally, remember, you are only in a class—don't take everything you hear or read as infallible truth. I do not want to instill in you a flippant attitude that dismisses your lectures and textbooks as probably false. No. You have much to learn from them. You should simply listen carefully and never change any *important* part of your thinking until you pursue further information. If something in a lecture or textbook makes you change from Democrat to Republican or from strong Christian beliefs to uncertain beliefs, you have changed too easily. You are being irrational to change fundamental beliefs on the basis of what you hear or read in classes. Fundamental beliefs should be changed only after long study in the library, consultation with many trusted and learned advisers, and sincere prayer for wisdom.

Classes and textbooks are introductions to knowledge. Your graduation is called "commencement" because it is a beginning. Your commencement symbolizes that you have been taught an introductory knowledge and are fully prepared to begin to pursue truth more deeply *after* you have graduated from college. The discovery of knowledge, the pursuit of truth and the attainment of wisdom make up a long pilgrimage. Never give up long-term goals and deep-seated understandings because of a one-semester class.

Useful Knowledge, But Is It True?

When modern universities limit the axioms normally allowed in a discipline, the goal is to make universities more useful to a broader range of people and societies. Christians may find this hard, because sometimes "useful" and "true" can be wrongly equated or confused. An astrophysicist recently told a journalist:

> You have to distinguish between the way we talk and the way we think when we reflect on it. Scientists have a shorthand for talking which leaves implicit a lot of assumptions. We may well talk as if we're interested in "the truth" but actually this is just a shorthand for something like "useful description" or "better approximation."

"Useful description" and "better approximation" *are* "the truth," or are they *instead of* "the truth"? Most people in the modern university leave the distinction rather vague. We pick the axioms and logical strategies that are the most likely to yield the most useful knowledge, while hoping that it is true as well.

Did you know that all the great questions of science have been answered? There is a perfectly rational answer to life, the universe and everything. It is called "occasionalism" and was best presented by a contemporary of Isaac Newton named Nicolas Malebranche in a book called *The Search After Truth.* As an example of how occasionalism answers scientific problems, let's look at the problem of sight and perception. Scientists still do not know how impulses recorded in the eye and transferred to the brain enter our consciousness and help us make decisions. We know a lot about both ends of the process but cannot figure out the middle step from brain cells to conscious perception. Occasionalism's answer is, God picks up the sense data in the brain cells and delivers it to our consciousness.

Great answer. It has a good chance of being the most true answer. It is the answer that occasionalism gives to almost every hard question: "God did it." God is the agent at work at every occasion, whether it be causing the earth to rotate, holding the nucleus of an atom together or delivering sense data from the brain to the mind. It is a perfectly rational answer and quite possibly is the ultimate truth. But today it is not considered good science, because it is not considered a "useful" answer. It does not help us make any further steps toward understanding causes in nature. I once heard a philosopher of science explain that Malebranche's occasionalism may be correct but it takes all the fun out of being a scientist.

A similar situation happens in my American history class. When studying the causes of the Civil War, I explain that Abraham Lincoln speculated in his second inaugural address that God caused the war as a retribution on both the North and the South for slavery. Lincoln may be right—God caused the war. However, such an answer is not "useful." The answer doesn't encourage further inquiry into the economic, political and cultural factors that contributed to secession. The answer is like a thousand-pound gorilla interrupting the class's discussion of developments before the war. I tell my students that if Lincoln were in my class and turned in his address as his paper, I would have to be severe with his grade.

It is one of the limits of modern academic history as taught in secular universities that "God did it" is not appreciated as an answer, even though it may be the ultimate truth. "God did it" is not considered a useful answer, and besides, it takes the fun out of being a historian. (In chapter ten I will describe how a student can study the God-did-it answer and get away with it.)

Description, Measurement and Knowledge
Sometimes you will encounter professors who don't understand the weaknesses, the tradeoffs and the limitations of university logic. It happens. Professors can be seduced by their own rhetoric. For example, remember I told you about the quote carved in stone over a door

at the University of Chicago? The quote is a shortened version of Kelvin's Dictum:

> When you can measure what you are speaking about, and express it in numbers, you know something about it; but when you cannot measure it, when you cannot express it in numbers, your knowledge is of a meagre and unsatisfactory kind.

Lord Kelvin, a nineteenth-century physicist, was overly excited about the possibilities of numbers and very confused about the meaning of "knowledge." Measurement is a wonderful tool, especially the use of statistics; however, it has its limits and certainly is not the highest knowledge.

You will meet professors who think that because they have a set of numbers to describe something or have described something so far as to give it a distinct name, they have done all that is necessary to proclaim "knowledge." Here again: listen carefully and ask deep questions.

No one knows what gravity is. We all know it exists. Isaac Newton's great feat was not to "discover" it, but rather to describe it with some useful numbers that are universally applicable. Newton's feat was great; however, he knew the limits of what he had done. G. W. von Leibniz, a rival, closely questioned him: But what *is* gravity? What *is* a "force"? Newton replied that he did not know—that maybe God was the force and gravity was some aspect of the way God works. Newton clearly stated that he did not know what gravity or forces *are;* rather, he had simply described the action in a way useful to anyone who can work the formula.

We still do not know what gravity is or what forces are. You will hear the term *forces* in every discipline, but no one knows what they actually are. Professors sometimes forget that useful description does not mean complete understanding. Feel free to question them on the deeper meaning of their words.

To sum up this section on Christians in the classroom, I have described three basic limitations that students should be aware of, ask questions about and listen for.

1. All of our logical construction of knowledge is built on axioms, assumptions rooted in our intuition. Paul in Romans 1 tells us God has put knowledge into us, so we Christians are comfortable with the idea of building on top of what we know deep within us. Secular universities are uncomfortable with axioms, especially axioms dealing with spiritual matters—such as our certainty that humans have souls. Disciplines at secular universities, therefore, try to use as few axioms as possible, and sometimes they add a few that seem dubious to you or me (such as the assumption that animal minds and human minds are the same). When we limit or expand the number of axioms, especially by excluding spiritual axioms, the number and type of conclusions available are limited.

2. All disciplines in modern universities avoid the God-did-it answer in an effort to be more useful. When scholars want to figure out how gravity works or the causes of the Civil War, "God does it" or "God did it" is not allowed as an answer, not because it is obviously false, but because it is not a useful answer. Useful answers are defined as answers that lead to further knowledge and encourage scholars to continue their research.

3. Professors can sometimes get confused about the limits of their knowledge. Describing and/or naming something does not mean full knowledge. We know much less than it sometimes appears.

The role of axioms at the beginnings of knowledge, the desire for the whole process of knowledge to focus on the useful, and the rhetorical confusions of knowledge are the three things students should contemplate. The first two are the rules of the game in secular universities. What Christian students must remember is that even though these rules have been successful in the last century, that does not mean that Christians have to abide by them at all times in universities. We Christians know some things—such as the existence of our souls and that God is actively involved in the world—that do not fit the rules. This does not mean that we are not correct, and it certainly does not mean that Christians are not as rational as non-Christian professors or students. It just means that Christian students need to understand that logic is a toolbox of strategies, and sometimes Christians use different tools from the ones normally used at universities. In a later chapter I will discuss how Christians can modify the rules.

— 9 —

The Mind-Boggling Life of Being Rational

All creation is wild. The stars, our minds, the behavior of plants, all of it is wild stuff. Being rational is often equated with being boring: being Mr. Spock instead of Captain Kirk. But rationality is really a wild roller-coaster ride full of upside-down swings, dark tunnels and dangerous leaps. Blaise Pascal, the Christian philosopher and mathematician with the computer language named after him, described one of rationalism's most wild twists: "There is nothing so consistent with reason as the denial of reason." Pascal used statements like this to shock readers into thinking bigger thoughts about rationalism. The mind and the soul for Pascal, as for most Christians throughout history, were one. There was no separation of heart and mind in the way we often talk about emotions and rationalism today. Rationalism in the fullest sense is a combination of strict reasoning, experience of creation, and introspective understanding of an individual's desires, memories and internal knowledge.

Pascal in his book of notes called *Pensées* was a master at making readers think about the large problems of being rational. In one passage Pascal pictured humans as suspended in a finite middle world between infinite bigness and infinite smallness. The infinities that sandwich us are part of the fullness of God's truth and are far beyond the small and fragile minds of humans. For Pascal, human rationalism, and especially university rationalism, is often misleading, because such limited rationalism can encourage people to be overconfident. Universities too often emphasize the finite middle area of rationalism rather than the infinite fullness of rationalism that sandwiches the finite. By emphasizing the finite and human, professors and students can sometimes forget the wildness of truth and the wildness of being truly rational people. University truths tend to be confined, whereas the truths that set us free are infinite and wild.

Wise Books and Wise People

Your best classes in college will probably be with professors who understand the wildness of rationality and the limitations of their scientific method. Einstein understood both, and there are professors at every college who understand both and who stretch the limitations by pushing on the edges of wildness in their classes. Some professors write books that reach beyond the classroom with their understanding that rationalism is much bigger than most university limits. Glenn Tinder is a political science professor whose recent writings demand that politics recognize its spiritual dimensions. Robert Coles is a prolific author and popular professor of psychology who embraces a much larger vision of the human soul than most psychologists. Rather than quoting other psychologists all the time, his books are mostly reports from children, social workers and other people who sense that being human is not just the sum of the chemical reactions in our body. Jeffrey Russell, one of my history professors, has written five volumes on the history of the devil and the way societies have viewed evil. I remember well being in his classes. He encouraged us to be rational in the larger sense that Pascal hoped for. He encouraged us to think about the wildness of being rational.

Cherish the professors who inspire wisdom and a wide view of rationality. Listen carefully and ask questions. Over the years the seeds planted in those classes can blossom into wisdom. But you have to nurture them. Pray for God to make you wise. Study the Bible. Study books beyond those merely assigned to you in class. Go to church where your ministers and fellow Christians can help you open your mind to the fullness of rationalism. Read biographies of wise Christians such as Pascal, and read what they themselves wrote, including Pascal's *Pensées.* The title makes it sound harder to read than it really is. *Pensées* just means "thoughts." A good introduction to Pascal and a wide view of being a rational Christian is *Making Sense of It All: Pascal and the Meaning of Life* by Thomas V. Morris, a philosophy professor at Notre Dame University. Morris has just published another useful book that collects the religious thoughts of important academic philosophers: *God and the Philosophers: The Reconciliation of Faith and Reason.* Another great book is *Fundamental Things Apply: Reflecting on Christian Basics* by Clyde Crews. Crews is a priest/professor at Bellarmine College, a Roman Catholic college across the river from where I teach. In the Louisville area Crews is well known as a model of the best kind of academic Christian: loving, rational, humble and devoted to his classes and community service.

Wise books and wise people are all around you. Don't waste the opportunity. Ask your minister to loan you some books. If you are interested in an author that I have mentioned, simply go to your library and punch his or her name into a computer catalog or database. Interlibrary loan will get you almost any book you want. Information and help are available. When I was a freshman in college I decided to read everything that C. S. Lewis had ever written. C. S. Lewis was a very wise Christian, and I learned a lot before giving up on ever trying to read *everything* he wrote.

Read and discuss! Read old books and new books. Find an author you trust and try to read everything he or she wrote. Talk to your minister. Ministers are usually broadly educated and are excited to talk with parishioners interested in books and ideas. If you have a wise minister, take him or her on as an intellectual advisor to help balance the advisors you have at the university. God wants you to have wisdom. Seek it and you will find it.

But what happens when your best classes and wisest professors point you in non-Christian directions? How is a Christian to handle truths that seem antagonistic to the faith? Truth is wild, and sometimes the wildness challenges our faith. Sometimes what seems true is not. Sometimes what is true makes no sense. Sometimes wisdom is found where we do not think it should be. Jesus, remember, often confounded those who followed him most closely. What is a Christian striving to be both rational and faithful to do? In the next chapter I offer three types of rational actions when your classes seem to be leading in an anti-Christian direction: (1) suspended decision, (2) accommodation and (3) appeal to authority.

Being Intellectually Honest

None of these entail renouncing Christianity. Some may say it is intellectually dishonest to not allow the option of renouncing Christianity as a fourth option and that by not allowing denial of Christianity as a possible response I have loaded the deck. However, a Christian who has experienced God's love, who knows deeply in his or her soul the breath of the Holy Spirit, who has reached out for Jesus' forgiveness and help, and who knows that Christianity unites life with all its love and anger, joy and sadness, simplicity and complexity cannot pretend that some information from some university classroom might outweigh what he or she knows so deeply. A Christian who has experienced the Truth cannot give up that inkling just because he or she gets stumped on a few questions at a university. Life is big, data is small. Life in Jesus is infinite, universities are finite. Trust in overwhelming knowledge is rational, trust in what you are told in a classroom merely reasonable.

Let me give an analogy: Am I being intellectually dishonest to say that no information learned at the university could possibly convince me that the love I have for my two sons does not exist as true love? I love my boys. I know it deeply. I know that love exists in a way that overwhelms me. I know that love is bigger than me.

My knowledge of the existence of love is not something vulnerable to a book or professor that tells me that love is just a chemical reaction in our bodies or some sort of self-preservation mechanism implanted in us through evolution. No data about hormones in my brain or an evolutionary theory is going to make me think that my love for my boys is simply the result of some biological necessity. I know a love in my heart that is too big for chemistry and hormones. I know I exist, I know the truth of this love, I know that something we call a heart, my spiritual center, exists, and every morning when I make breakfast for my boys I know the object of that love in my heart. No scientific study demonstrating a high probability can tip the balance of my reason against the solid weight of such a knowledge. I know a love that cannot be reduced to physiology.

Just like the truth of a father's love for his children, the truth of Jesus' love for us also has too much weight to ever be tipped on the balance of scientific probabilities. Christians know deeply to whom they belong. It would be a stupid word game to pretend that a class, a professor or some accumulation of data might require a Christian to renounce his or her Christianity.

I suggest that every reader put down this book now and confirm the depth of their knowledge of the love of Jesus before going on. Why are you a Christian? Maybe you have doubts about parts of Christian doctrine. Set those aside for now. What do you know deeply? As the revival hymn says:

> Just as I am, though tossed about
> With many a conflict, many a doubt;
> Fightings and fears within, without,
> O Lamb of God, I come, I come.

We come because we know something deeper than our doubts. What do you know at the deepest core of your faith? Most people are sure there is a Creator God. The world around us is so orderly, and so much in our lives seems to have a purpose. But what of Jesus? How could he be both man and God? Dying on a cross and rising from the grave may seem remote, like a fairy story. It does to me sometimes, but it most often makes sense to me in a large way. If you have doubts, join with your fellow Christians and share knowledge and experiences. Talk to your minister. Most importantly, read your Bible and pray every day. Communicate with God. Pray for wisdom. The book of James says that if anyone lacks wisdom, he or she can ask God for it.

My purpose here is very limited. My book is about how to handle being a Christian in the midst of secular universities. If you first have questions about the faith itself, then know that you need to work those out. Read on—some of the things I write may help—but remember that I am taking the strength of the reader's knowledge for granted.

With that said, we can move on in the next three chapters to the basic ways Christians can handle information presented to them in classes that seem antagonistic to their faith.

— 10 —

Decisions
Waiting,
Accommodating
& Appealing
to Authority

The application of reason to data helps us build good lives and gain greater understanding of creation. Universities are enormously helpful in society because they produce so much data, so much information, so much new knowledge. Universities are also helpful in creating a consensus of reasonable data analysis. Rationality, however, is bigger than data and the reasonable analysis of data.

Waiting

Albert Einstein was a great scientist because he did not overrate data and being reasonable. He relied heavily on his intuition. He *felt* deep within himself that his theories—theories such as time slows down when you approach the speed of light—were true even though they seemed absurd and unreasonable.

Even a decade or so after Einstein first published his ideas, few scientists could understand what he had written, but bits and pieces of new information increasingly confirmed his theories. Another decade later he was the most famous scientist on earth and was revered as a genius. What Einstein had *felt* was true had turned out to *be* true.

Younger physicists picked up on some of Einstein's ideas and developed a new science called quantum physics. To their shock, the young scientists found that Einstein didn't follow them into quantum physics. They still considered him a genius and competed for the chance to be near him; however, once again Einstein was refusing to overrate data and its reasonable analysis. Einstein's intuition refused to allow him to believe the new quantum physics which described the universe as chaotic and full of random chance. He wrote that an "inner voice tells me" that the new physics was not the whole story. At sixty-five years of age, Einstein wrote to a friend and intellectual opponent:

> You believe in the God who plays dice, and I in complete law and order in the world, which objectively exists, and which I, in a wildly speculative way, am trying to capture. I firmly believe, but I hope that someone will discover a more realistic way, or rather a more tangible basis than it has been my lot to do. Even the great initial success of the quantum theory does not make me believe in the fundamental dice game, although I am well aware that our younger colleagues interpret this as a consequence of senility.

Einstein was consistent at the beginning of his career and at the end. He worked hard. He read the new data. He listened to the reasonable analysis of new data by other physicists. He was a conscientious scientist. He was not the sort of academic who happens to have one good idea and then sits back on it the rest of his life. Einstein understood that rationality was bigger than being reasonable with the data. Like Pascal he was willing to abandon reason when it was outweighed by his informed intuition. It worked when he was young. He held on to the method when he was old. In his youth he was able to scientifically convince the world that his intuition was right. In old age, however, he could not find the scientific means necessary to convince other physicists that his intuition was true.

Einstein practiced suspended decision-making. For the last half of his life he was sure something was wrong with the data and its analysis. He could not prove it though. When other physicists confronted him and asked him to submit to the data, Einstein said, "Wait." He needed more time to study the situation. He needed more time to try to prove his own theory. He refused to be forced into what he considered a rash decision.

As a student, do not allow yourself to be forced into thinking that you have to decide whether Christianity or any other important aspect of your life must rise or fall because of the information you learn in a class. Don't be flippant. Don't be irrational. Just remember that being rational is much bigger than making immediate decisions based on a limited amount of data. Being rational often demands suspending one's decisions or conclusions until one's intuition comes into line with the knowledge one is accumulating—or knowledge comes into line with intuition.

This is maybe the most practical advice I can give: *don't let any one class at the university change the way you think about an important aspect of your life.* A number of classes over a long period of time may help you rethink some important things, but don't let one semester change your life. If you learn something so big that you think your life *must* change and must change *quickly,* then make sure you consult with many trusted advisers.

John Henry Newman was one of the most rational and conscientious decision-makers in history. In 1845, after over a decade of study, prayer and discussion, Newman switched from the Church of England to the Roman Catholic Church. To us this might not seem like much, but nineteenth-century England treated Roman Catholics much like Americans used to treat communists. Newman lost his teaching job at Oxford. He lost many friends. He was a famous man who suddenly became infamous.

Let me give a long quote from Newman. You may have to read it a few times, but it is worth the effort.

My argument is in outline as follows: that that absolute certitude which we [are] able to possess, whether as to the truths of natural theology, or as to the fact of a revelation, [is] the result of an assemblage of concurring and converging probabilities, and that, both according to the constitution of the human mind and the will of its Maker; that certitude [is] a habit of mind, that certainty [is] a quality of propositions; that probabilities which [do] not reach to logical certainty, might create a mental certitude; that the certitude thus created might equal in measure and strength the certitude which was created by the strictest scientific demonstration; and that to have such certitude might in given cases and to given individuals be a plain duty, though not to others in other circumstances.

I know this is hard to read. Stretch your mind by wrestling with this paragraph like you would an algebra problem. Tear it apart and put it back together.

Newman is offering you confidence. When you are studying science or philosophy or anthropology late some evening with a group of classmates, and they tell you that if you were "honestly open-minded" you would see that your Christianity cannot hold up to the "facts," know that by keeping your Christianity you are being honest to "an assemblage of concurring and converging probabilities" that involve your whole rational being. If your friends raise doubts, talk more with them and seek more information; but don't lose confidence in the rationality of Christianity.

It took Newman a decade to gather enough information to switch churches! "Great acts take time," he explained. Go slow with any big decision—especially those involving your Christianity. There is no need to rush major decisions. Allow time for your mental certitude to develop. Pray and seek advice from ministers, teachers and friends, knowing that God wants to help you make the best decision. God is active.

Einstein was a genius, yet he never could gather enough information to offset or prove his intuition. If Einstein had ever read Newman's book, he would have agreed with the passage quoted above.

Rationality is a convergence of knowledge from many different sources to which the tools of logic are applied in the hope of organizing that knowledge to conform as closely as possible to truth. It takes time. Enjoy the process.

Mysteries

Another of Newman's great lines goes something like this: Numerous difficulties don't necessarily add up to a doubt. Mysteries are all around us. Don't let the mysteries drag you down into oppressive doubting. Mysteries just remind us that we are finite. "Be comforted, small one, in your smallness."

On some issues you may have to wait until you see God face to face. As Pascal noted, sometimes it is reasonable to abandon reason. That's a great line! Let it swim awhile in your brain: *Sometimes it is reasonable to abandon reason.* Isaiah tells us that God's ways are not necessarily our ways. God's answers to Job's questions are nonanswers: "Where were you when I created the universe?" Paul says that we see through a glass darkly now, but someday we'll see face to face.

All reasonable people and any rational perspective on the pursuit of knowledge must admit that there are more mysteries than facts, more things unknown than known, more things misunderstood than understood. Universities are centers of disseminating information and misinformation. Universities rarely advertise their lack of information. Professors and students have done an excellent job at discovering lots of truths—especially figuring out how physical things work. Once they figure out how things work, then professors and students do an excellent job at fiddling with things in order to make them work for us. Medical professors fiddle with the human body and have done a great job. Physicists fiddle with atoms and such and have also done a great job—even to the point of being able to blow us all up. But doctors don't know what life is, and physicists don't know what gravity is. Remember, the status of all knowledge at universities is summed up in the cartoon of the formula on the chalkboard with the two sides of the equation connected by "(a miracle happens here)."

The university is filled with knowledge, but all of it has more holes in it than we like to admit. Rational living keeps the reasonable analysis of the best data woven tightly with your intuition. When they cannot be woven together, suspend judgment while pursuing the problem further. Like Einstein you may leave this mortal life still having some problems hanging unanswered. That's okay. You're only human. Be comforted in your smallness.

Accommodation

Accommodation is the give-and-take between new knowledge and old knowledge. Remember from the previous chapter that both Christianity and universities believe in the progress of knowledge—that new knowledge can be discovered and better understandings of the cosmos and humanity can be constructed. We Christians believe that God, primarily through the work of the Holy Spirit, wants to help humanity discover new knowledge and construct better understandings. Often the help of the Holy Spirit involves guiding the accommodation of a new understanding with an old understanding.

One such accommodation is described in Acts 11, where it is reported that the apostles received information that Gentiles were converting to Christianity. This information had to be dealt with. Many of the Christians still insisted on the old Jewish separation from the Gentiles. Acts says that though many had their doubts, the Holy Spirit convinced them that "God has granted life-giving repentance to the Gentiles also."

Christians must have open minds. Sometimes new knowledge is false or just a passing intellectual phase. Not all new knowledge is to be accommodated. Some should be rejected, some accommodated provisionally and some fully. Sometimes Christians should just wait and see if the new knowledge holds up over time before they decide what to do with it.

Psychoanalysis

One of the great accommodation debates of the twentieth century is over the validity and usefulness of Freudian and Jungian psychoanalysis. Psychoanalysis is a rational science—a Yale professor who wrote a biography of Freud insists that psychoanalysis is a science like calculus—but universities generally avoid psychoanalysis because it has a large number of extra axioms. (Remember, public universities try to limit the number of axioms.) Psychology departments usually avoid psychoanalysis (except some of the personality tests derived from Jung). Those who seem most committed to it are in the fields of fine arts, literature, film studies and gender studies. Christian seminaries are often intrigued with psychoanalysis, but rank-and-file Christians are wary of it.

Both Freudian and Jungian forms of psychoanalysis are rooted in anti-Christian ideas. Sigmund Freud developed one form of psychoanalysis that tries to explain almost everything people think and do in terms of sexual influences on the unconscious. Carl Jung developed the other, which has less emphasis on sex and is much more mystical and seemingly religious. Jung insisted that humans are connected unconsciously to each other and to fundamental myths or archetypes. Jung is very hard to pin down; however, for both men, Christianity was created by humans rather than being a revelation from God.

For example, the importance of Mary, the virgin mother of Jesus, is explained away as either the result of sexual urges or as one among many manifestations of a virgin archetype and a mother archetype. Christians believe that Mary is important because God made her important. Mary, inspired by the Holy Spirit, upon hearing the news of her pregnancy declared that "all generations will count me blessed" (Lk 1:48). Psychoanalysis in its pure form as developed by Freud and Jung dissects the truth of Mary and destroys her blessedness.

Certainly Freudian and Jungian psychoanalysis in their most strict forms should be rejected by Christians; however, there seems to be some truth in some of the things these men said. Freud was right that sexual urges do influence our lives. Jung wrote in his *Memories, Dreams, Reflections* that he wanted psychiatry to be a bridge between the spiritual and material world. Psychiatry would be an academic study where myths and archetypes would be treated more seriously than they are in academic psychology. Jung was right about the need to treat myths and archetypes more seriously. Because Freud and Jung were right about some things, universities and seminaries struggle with accommodating them.

As for me, I don't know. Maybe psychoanalysis is a hundred-year fad that will pass when better information is available. Maybe it is an inkling of a better understanding of humanity.

Should you accommodate some aspects of psychoanalysis into your Christianity? I suggest you enjoy the debate. Think hard. Read books. Struggle with the problem. Admit any truths or partial truths you find. Ask questions. Ask your minister too. Most ministers had to think about Jung in seminary. Pray. Ask for the Holy Spirit's guidance.

If the Holy Spirit seems to give you guidance, then test that guidance. When the Holy Spirit confirms the truth of new knowledge that should be accommodated into Christianity, the breath of inspiration can come to one person; however, nothing should be confidently incorporated into Christianity unless *many* people feel the same breath of inspiration from the Holy Spirit. Test what you think the Holy Spirit confirms by discussing it with trusted Christian friends and advisers. Remember you are in a race to pursue knowledge, but you are in an unbroken circle too. Christianity is a community of knowledge. Individualism and freedom are always to be rooted in communal respect. Accommodation is most strong as a communal enterprise. An individual who makes an accommodation against the weight of community advice is on intellectual thin ice.

Biological Evolution

Aside from psychoanalysis, biological evolution is an accommodation problem for Christians. Like psychoanalysis, biological evolution in its strictest form is anti-Christian. Strict biological evolution describes mechanisms of change through time that are purposeless. There is no divine guidance and no goal. Humans are merely animals struggling to have their species survive, just like any other living thing. Humans are not even the "fittest" in the "survival of the fittest." Beetles are more "fit" than us to survive.

Christians must reject such a strict form of biological evolution. God created us for a purpose, and God is active in all creation. However, there seems to be much truth in some theories of evolution. In the last hundred years, many parts of the various theories of evolution have been adopted by some Christians. Essentially those Christians look for the hand of God in evolution. Some Christians want to repress all discussion of possible accommodation. Those Christians are just as wrong as those on the biology faculty at San Francisco State who are trying to repress one of their biologists from teaching that there might have been an "intelligent agent" active in creation. There is a good chance the theories of evolution are wrong; however, repressing accommodation is not the way to advance toward truth. Only open minds making open inquiries can ever hope to synthesize the data into a better theory.

Some secular university professors, because they separate religion and knowledge in their lives, cannot understand why Christians feel threatened by the theory of biological evolution. They also don't understand why many Christians think that the evolutionists are close-minded and paranoid when they refuse to allow any thought of divine activity or "intelligent agent" to be discussed in class. Stephen Jay Gould, a professor at Harvard and famous essayist on scientific subjects, wrote, "Science simply cannot (by its legitimate methods) adjudicate the issue of God's possible superintendence of nature. We neither affirm nor deny it; we simply can't comment on it as scientists."

Evolutionary scientists—including Gould—need to realize that we Christians don't find them not commenting. Phillip E. Johnson, a Christian law professor at Berkeley, wrote a book that Gould attacked, *Darwin on Trial.* Johnson responded to Gould's attack by quoting from one of Gould's own articles. "No intervening spirit," wrote Gould, "watches lovingly over the affairs of nature. . . . And whatever we think of God, his existence is not manifest in the products of nature." It is hard to imagine how Gould thinks he is only making a scientific statement that makes no comment on Christianity!

Too many scientists have separated their academic life from the rest of their life. In their minds they think they can talk science talk and not have it affect the way people walk. Their biggest error in the classroom is to think that their students have disassociated science from life in the way they have. They think their science lectures should not leak over into the religious lives of their students. Good students do not cut their lives into compartments in the manner of some of their professors, and they will relate their science classes to all the rest of their classes.

A good student who is a Christian will have to reject the anti-God aspects of evolutionary theories because of what a Christian knows deeply and fully in the soul. We have *experienced* God's active involvement in our life. As rational beings we weigh the evidence: an unguided evolution with no end purpose is impossible because it does not fit with our experience of God, with our experience of nature and with the experience of the majority of people both past and present.

Having noted that some of the most strict aspects of evolutionary theories will have to be rejected, be glad that there is a wide-open field of evolutionary theories and facts that Christians can possibly accommodate into their understanding of how God the Creator works. Nature is wonderfully complex. It has the imprint of God in it. Maybe the evolutionary scientists have much to teach us about God but don't know it.

Slippage

But watch out for slippage. Scientists such as Gould fall into slippage often, and the wary student must separate what must be accommodated from what does not have to be accommodated. Slippage is what Gould is doing in the two quotes above. Good scientists, of whom Gould is one, are usually careful to state that modern science is a method, not a conclusion. The "legitimate methods" he cites that make no claim one way or the other about the existence of God are the most scientists stick to in their research. The slippage occurs when the science-as-method of scientists slips into our cultural veneration of the conclusions promulgated by science professors. In the first quote Gould is talking as a scientist. In the second quote he is talking as a science professor about his own conclusions.

Slippage. Gould does not seem to recognize that his work as a scientist is different from his work as an insightful and popular science professor. Watch out for slippage in your classes. We Christians are only required to deal with the results of good scientific method. We are not required to accommodate the personal theories and promulgations that professors draw from their work as scientists.

Let me explain more fully. It is very important that we understand what we are required to accommodate and what we are not. What follows is a simplified description of three categories of rationality at universities. You, as a student, are required to accommodate only the material in the middle category.

Category A	**Category B**	**Category C**
axioms	scientific method	conclusions
self-evident truths	discovery of facts	theories
the obvious	data	interpretations
intuitions	normal mathematics	speculations
internal experience	measurement	
initial assumptions	demonstrations such as	
	A=B, B=C,	
	therefore A=C	

Most university professors use all three of the categories, and their work can be described as A+B=C. In chapter eight I explained how most professors try to use as few axioms as possible—they want to work as little as possible in category A. The most fun work is in category C, formulating exciting conclusions. The hardest work is in category B. Most professors, whether biologists, sociologists, historians or even philosophers, work as much as possible in category B.

The more work we do in category B, the better our conclusions in category C. A strong C is the goal, but to get there a professor must join some material from category A with much work in category B.

When Professor Gould tells us that science cannot judge whether there is a God, he says this from within category B. But when he tells us that "there is no God watching lovingly over the affairs of nature," he is working in category C by assuming an axiom from category A. He has slipped from B to C by way of A.

Evolutionists who point to the fact that beak shapes change through generations of birds according to their environment are working in category B. When they then insist that natural selection is a mechanism that works without God, they have adopted an axiom from A and have moved into C. A historian who shows you the evidence that Emperor Constantine was directly involved in the Council of Nicea, where the theological description of the Trinity was decided, is working in category B. If the historian then insists that the Trinity is the result of a political decision, that historian has moved into C by way of A.

You as a student are never required to accommodate ideas presented to you from category A or C. You are, however, required to deal conscientiously and rationally with information from category B.

Don't Put God in a Box
Be wary, but don't be antagonistic. Trust the Holy Spirit. Pray for wisdom. Listen carefully. Study hard. Accommodation can be learning at its best as part of the way God continues to teach us. Of course your Christianity cannot be revised every time you learn something new in class. Christianity cannot be just a conglomeration of compromises with whatever passing fad is being promulgated at universities. But God doesn't want closed minds either.

When I was thirteen years old, I tried to nail an older and wiser seventeen-year-old Christian on some fine point of theology. He responded, "Don't put God in a box." He was right. God is infinite, and we are finite. Open-minded Christians, praying regularly for wisdom and more knowledge, must find the narrow way between accepting whatever new knowledge is fashionable in universities and locking God into a box.

A warning: one of the important arguments against evolution that I have often heard and read (my mom and dad were very antagonistic to the idea of evolution when I was growing up) is that there is no evidence for evolution from one species to another. There is plenty of evidence for butterflies changing color or finches developing different beaks, but there is no evidence of changes from one type of living thing to another type.

At a dinner party with a colleague who is a non-Christian evolutionary biologist, I asked about this problem. He had a complex but good answer. The Christian argument is right if you define *species* in the traditional way; however, "species" is a tough concept to define in modern biology. Most modern biologists use genetics to define "speciation," or the creation of species. Genetics does provide evidence of one species evolving into another species.

My friend and I talked further about the ways God could be involved in evolution. I learned a lot as he cooked and I stood next to him in the kitchen. Talking with him about the careful definition of terms, I realized that much of the fight between antievolutionist Christians and non-Christian evolutionists is debate gone awry. The debaters are constantly misunderstanding each other's terms. Words like *species* are used in different ways.

Also some Christians think that if you poke one hole in a theory of evolution, then all evolutionary theories fall. This is not true. I asked my friend if he ever saw a time when evolution could be superseded by a completely different theory. "Sure," he said. He wasn't dogmatic. He said that the best theories explain maybe 60 or 70 percent of the information, and lesser theories explain maybe 20 or 30 percent. Accumulation of new information can cause the lesser theories to increase in their percentage and the best theories to decrease. At some point the balance can tip.

Good science and good debate leads us to be open-minded and to attempt to carefully understand each other's terms and perspectives. Christianity at its best is never close-minded and is always seeking good communication.

If new information is true, if new information doesn't contradict the great truths we know in our souls, if it explains a high percentage of things otherwise unexplainable, then, even if new information stretches our understanding of Christianity, we should accommodate it. If we are thinking people, we will be wrestling always with new information. As always: pray, ask questions, trust wise advisers and pursue the truth. We know that no true information can contradict the great unifying Truth that is in God.

Another warning: do not reject any information with the statement "God wouldn't do it that way." Such a statement does not take seriously the God of the Bible. Who knows fully the mind and will of God? God warns us in Isaiah that "my thoughts are not your thoughts nor are your ways my ways" (Is 55:8).

My mother will let me tell this story about her. When I was first in college, evolution came up for debate around the dinner table. My brothers, my dad and I were loudly debating when my mother announced over the din: "I am not related to an orangutan!" It was a great family moment, and her sons have not let her forget the outburst.

The trouble with such a statement, however, is that it was my mom's way of saying, "God would not do it that way." Isaiah warns us about such presumption. Before evolutionary theories began to dominate science in the nineteenth century, Thomas Jefferson and many eighteenth-century scientists believed very strongly in a theory of nature that insisted that species *never* become extinct. When they discovered fossils, they insisted that that fish or animal *must* still exist somewhere in the world. Why did they insist this? Because "God would not do it that way." They insisted that God, being perfect, created a perfect system of nature. If a species died off, the system of nature would be imperfect. God would have been "uneconomical" to create things only to have them go extinct.

But all the evidence we have now makes it absurd to think that some species do not die off. Does it mean God is no longer a perfect Creator? No. It just means God's thoughts and ways were not necessarily Jefferson's.

When we accommodate new information into our lives, especially information that may stretch our understanding of the way God works, we are striving to be humble. We must not accommodate every bit of seeming information. That would be pride. It would be prideful of us humans to make our understanding of God conform to university knowledge. However, to accommodate bits of knowledge that carry great weight of evidence is humility. It is the humility of understanding our smallness as we seek to know more about God and creation.

Appealing to Authorities

Waiting and accommodation are two of the three responses to challenging information in your classes. Appealing to authorities is the third and last. The great myth of modern society is that people think better if they think for themselves. We are constantly encouraged to "question authority." Everyone in college is taught the model of René Descartes, the philosopher who threw off Aristotle and all of what he was told and sat down in an inn in 1619 to figure everything out for himself. To begin he had to doubt everything, even his own existence. After proving his existence with "I think, therefore I am," he moved on to become the father of modern individualistic thinking. The myth of Descartes, that we must think for ourselves, is a mirage. It is not completely false but is very misleading.

Everybody lives by shared information. Everybody accepts authorities. The university exists for corporate thinking, not individual thinking. How could knowledge accumulate if people were just thinking for themselves? Honesty is such an important value in universities because our work is mostly based on trust. Experimental scientists trust the experiments they read about. Historians trust the quotes and footnotes in the books they use. Scholars recognize that there have been cases of fraud in every discipline, but professors would never have time to learn anything new if they were constantly checking all the work done by their sources. Universities are primarily founded on trusting authority, not questioning authority. Descartes never doubted everything. Your professors serve two roles: they are explorers on the frontiers of knowledge, while at the same time they are librarians cataloging and guarding the knowledge handed down by the authorities of the past.

As a student, feel free to trust authorities. Do so wisely, but do not think that trusting is irrational or unscientific. Books and professors are authorities in the areas of their expertise. Trust them to give you the best information available in the field. There is an ancient tradition in logic, taught prominently by Quintilian and Augustine and being revived by some modern academic philosophers, that there is no dishonor in trusting a trustworthy authority. No dishonor. Think about it. It means that we might be wrong; however, we are still being rational. As small and finite humans we are doing the best we can. Trusting trustworthy sources is essential to being rational.

The Bible as Credible Testimony

The most important authority for us Christians is the Bible. It is a book we trust. Our trust is rational, and it is not misplaced. The Bible is especially a good authority in the field of history. There are many events taught in history classes that are only known from the Bible. About a hundred years ago, the testimony of the Bible as to historical events and places was not much accepted in universities. Archaeologists, however, have led the way in showing academics that many events and places in the Bible can be verified. The trustworthiness of the Bible as a historical source keeps increasing. As a historian, I can tell you that almost everything we know about Jesus comes from the Bible, and academic historians find no dishonor in trusting the Bible's testimony about his birth, travels, ethical teachings and death. Most academic historians, however, arbitrarily choose not to trust the testimony of miracles and the resurrection, but it is my opinion that they do so irrationally (that is, they are being inconsistent).

Historians justify bypassing testimony of miracles by loose use of a bad theory. The bad theory involves balancing possibilities in which supernatural events are arbitrarily ruled so improbable that they rank as impossible for historians to justify. Philosophers have long pointed out the problems with our theory, but we historians continue to use it superficially as a means to avoid dealing with the amazingly large amount of credible testimony that miracles have been regularly occurring throughout history.

Trust me. The Bible and thousands of other historical sources are full of credible testimony (from authorities that we can trust) that God has been active through history reaching out to humans through miracles.

I know a professor who loves his students and works hard for them, but he also is extremely antagonistic to Christianity. He will believe *anything* bad or stupid he hears about Christians or Christianity while refusing to trust any source to the contrary. In classes he spouts off about how irrational it is for Bible believers to think that the earth is 4004 years old. I told him that very few Bible believers think that the earth is 4004 years old—but that doesn't matter to him. At a dinner party where the subject of Christianity in public schools came up, he announced out of nowhere that "scholars now think that the body of Jesus was eaten by dogs." I suspect he announces such things in class regularly. What you should always remember is that we Christians have trustworthy sources. We have a rational trust in credible sources. There is no dishonor or irrationality in our trust of the Bible's account of Jesus' birth, life, death and resurrection. Speaking of Jesus' transfiguration, 2 Peter 1:16 reminds us, "It was not on tales, however cleverly concocted, that we relied when we told you about the power of our Lord Jesus Christ and his coming; rather with our own eyes we had witnessed his majesty."

Just as it is rational to accept the story of Socrates' life and death on the basis of the testimony of trustworthy reporters, so too it is rational to accept the story of Jesus' birth, life, death and resurrection. Rational living demands trust.

At one point I thought being an academic historian meant that I had to avoid using the clear testimony of the Bible about supernatural events. I wanted to be a respectable historian. Once at UCSB I was eating donuts with a couple of students and a professor, Abraham Friesen, a Mennonite. He and one of the students were talking about using the Bible as an authority in historical scholarship, and I interrupted, declaring that it couldn't be done. I said we can believe the Bible as Christians, but as historians we must disallow the Bible's testimony about spiritual events.

I was wrong. It took me years to realize, but any consistent logic used by historians must demand that they weigh the testimony of all reported events, spiritual or not, with standard rules. If standard rules are applied consistently, then many of the stories of God's intervention in history have just as much credibility as many other often accepted stories. A student of mine helped me finally realize this.

Individualistic Rationalism Is a Myth

Historians know they have to rely on other people's accounts of events, but all academics need to be reminded that individualistic rationalism is a myth. If not a myth, it is at least an abstract ideal that has never happened in any human life. Modern universities preach the myth of thinking for oneself, but they forget that equal emphasis should be placed on trusting the right authorities. The man who is often proclaimed the father of modern philosophy is Descartes, the I-think-therefore-I-am man. Descartes began his process of thinking by trying to rely only on his own mind. He didn't really. Descartes relied on his Christian conception of God, on the rational methods and traditional antiskepticism strategies of Plato and Augustine, and on ideas and information he had gained from years of studying other people's books.

Individualism is good and can be helpful within careful boundaries, but I have a better model for you: Augustine. He inspired Descartes; however, he did not try to avoid trusting others. Modern university professors usually want to go as far as they can in their own minds before they begin to trust other people for information. Augustine started with his own mind but understood that, as a rational Christian, he had to *immediately* start trusting ideas and information from other people, from credible writings such as the Scriptures and from the testimony of his own senses. Augustine had great wisdom about his own sinfulness and intellectual weaknesses. He knew he needed God, the Bible, the church, creeds, other people and careful use of his senses in order to keep his mind on the right track. I recommend Augustine's books *On the Trinity, On the Profit of Believing* and *Handbook on Faith, Hope and Love.* These three works wonderfully show how Augustine merged introspection, his senses and credible testimony from the authorities of philosophy and Christianity.

Waiting, Accommodating and Trusting Authorities

I have so far offered three rational strategies for Christians in class who hear information that seems to contradict their Christianity. The first strategy is to suspend judgment until you have enough information to make a clear decision of truth or falsehood. Every rational person should suspend judgment until they have enough information to make a clear decision. The second strategy is accommodation. If information delivered in class stretches the edges of your understanding of Christianity but carries enough weight of evidence for you to conclude that it is true, then you should accommodate the new information into your understanding of Christianity. The third strategy of appealing to authority is necessary for both of the first two strategies to be rational. When you suspend judgment, you must begin to appeal to authorities for more information. When you accommodate information, you do so because of the weight of evidence and support of authorities. The rational student is not a lone ranger; the rational student is a member of a community of rational thinkers. A rational student trusts the wisdom of those worthy of trust.

Who are your authorities? Whom do you trust? I have trusted some professors, some friends and some ministers. When I had doubts or confusions, I asked for help. The church is an authority. The communion of saints past and present has built an institution with the guidance of the Holy Spirit. The church has many manifestations and is often not unified on any specific issue; however, overall the word of the church should have authority over us. The Bible is an authority.

Seeking authorities to help work out a problem or remove a doubt does not mean that we lose individuality or individual responsibility. Seeking authorities is simply an acknowledgment that we are stronger when we hold hands in the circle than when we are thinking alone. One mind is weaker than many.

Christianity is meant for the classroom. Christianity is part of your rationality. The classroom is where we enhance our knowledge, improve our rationality and test our wisdom. 1 Peter 1:13 tells us our "minds must be stripped for action and fully alert." Imprint that command on your mind, and be ready to pursue truth when you walk into class. Secular universities are wonderful places where you will find comrades in the pursuit of truth. You will find professors full of information and some with wisdom.

Do not hide your Christianity. Don't keep it in a box, separate from your studies. Learn to work with your faith within the context of class. Practice. You will find, I think, that non-Christians at the university will respect your Christianity if they know you have an open mind full of love for the truth.

–11–

The Bible in Class

Interpretation of the Bible is divisive. Christian unity is often destroyed when Christians debate the meaning and application of Scripture with the goal of conquering the opposition. Would that we all listened to Christ's prayer for unity in John 17 with hearts full of humility and love.

One of the greatest benefits for Christians attending a secular university is that they are encouraged to emphasize their unity with other Christians rather than their differences. Serious Christians at secular universities tend to realize they are a minority and on the same team.

The Bible often appears in university classes as literature or history but not as divine revelation. All Christians (I think) agree that the Bible is divine revelation. We also agree that it is a collaboration between God and humans. To some extent it is a human book. (Here again,

Christians too often divide and fight over the amount of human influence in the book.) Whatever its human components, the Bible includes God's communication with us.

Aside from the collaboration of God with humanity in the words of Scripture, the Bible is also closely tied with the history of the first Christian churches. The Bible is the church's as much as the church is the Bible's. By this I mean that in history the Bible and the church were being formed at the same time in the early centuries following the resurrection of Christ. There were other writings circulating among Christians that were not chosen to be part of the Bible. The churches had a significant hand in choosing what texts became our Bible. The Bible, in turn, played a significant role in guiding the development of the churches. It's a chicken and egg problem. We Christians believe that the Holy Spirit was active in guiding the creation of the Bible and the institutional church at the same time.

The result of having the Bible so closely interwoven with humans and the development of the church is confusion and debate. Christianity is complex while at the same time simple. Christians divide constantly over complexities. I recommend you focus on the simple: that the Bible is a gift from God which you must read regularly with humility and an open mind.

Christianity at Secular Universities
Secular universities usually do not divide over the Bible. They simply rank the Bible as one of the important human documents in world history. The Bible is usually taught in classes as a social phenomenon, historical influence, human philosophy and/or storehouse of human myths and symbols. There is pressure in secular universities not to teach the Bible as a divine book with special authority.

Many religious-minded professors feel pressure from their peers to avoid discussing Christianity as a "good" religion and possibly true. The federal courts also get in the act of selectively repressing discussion of religion. In *Bishop* v. *Aronov,* a recent case against a teacher at the University of Alabama who freely expressed his opinions in favor of Christianity and offered to meet with interested students after class, the federal courts ruled that "the university classroom is not an 'open forum' but rather a restricted venue dedicated to a specific educational purpose." A lower court rightfully noted that the University of Alabama was very selective in repressing discussion of religion. It allows philosophy classes to discuss whether a Supreme Being exists and political science classes to discuss whether religion is the "opiate of the people"; however, a physical education professor who encouraged students to attend his *optional* lecture on "Evidences of God in Human Physiology" is suppressed.

Such is the situation as it stands on most campuses and in the federal courts. There is pressure to avoid serious and positive discussion of Christianity. The possible divine authority of the Bible is generally believed to be out-of-bounds.

You will be glad to know that there are many Christian professors who do not give in to such vague pressure from peers and the courts, and there are many secular universities where Christian professors have the respect of their peers. I am happy to report to you that I feel *no* pressure from my peers at Indiana University Southeast to downplay my Christianity. Open-minded professors, administrators and judges know that Christianity is a rationally valid perspective on the cosmos which deserves to be openly discussed along with other perspectives, religions and philosophies. Just as my atheist friends should be free to present their view of the cosmos in a rational and positive way, religious professors deserve the same right. Professors have more than a right, they have a responsibility to be open and honest with students as they together pursue the truth.

Devout Professors on the Offensive

You will also be glad to know that in the national press there are a few professors standing up for equal rights for Christians in secular universities. Three leading voices to look for are Alvin Plantinga and George Marsden, who teach at Notre Dame, and Nicholas Wolterstorff at Yale. (Notre Dame, of course, is not a secular university and is leading a Christian academic synthesis in philosophy and history.) These critics of the double standard have been receiving media attention. In 1993 *The New York Times* reported on Marsden's call for universities to be more open-minded about Christianity. The May 4, 1994, issue of *The Chronicle of Higher Education* pictured him on the cover for a story titled "Devout Professors on the Offensive." The essence of Marsden's argument, and the argument of many Christian faculty, is that religious ways of knowing are no more subjective than any other way of knowing; therefore religious ways of knowing should be allowed freedom in a public university. Marsden's recent book, published by Oxford University Press, is called *The Soul of the American University: From Protestant Establishment to Established Nonbelief,* and in it he studies the history of the role of religious belief in leading secular universities. We Christians cannot demand control of public universities in the way we did a hundred and fifty years ago; however, Christians and other religious taxpayers and students can demand at least a rightful place in public education.

Wendell Berry, a University of Kentucky professor and a poet, novelist, essayist and popular advocate for a simplified, agrarian American economy, writes:

> Obviously, this issue of the Bible in the public schools cannot be resolved by federal court decisions that prescribe teaching methods. It can only be settled in terms of the freedom of teachers to teach as they believe and in terms of the relation of teachers and schools to their local communities.

Berry's complaint about how the Bible is taught is not narrowly Christian. Like any good professor he wants all the subjects taught in classrooms to be free to speak with all the power inherent in them. In terms of teaching literature, he wants to free all literature courses from repression: "We teach Bible 'as literature' on the quaint assumption that 'as literature' it will have no power over us. We do the same with Dante and Shakespeare and Milton as literature too—to deny their power to compel and challenge belief."

Truth has power, and the best professors and universities give that power, in whatever form, free rein in all classrooms.

The Bible should be free to work its powerful ways among all the rest that gets discussed and studied at secular universities. Never forget that the Bible is more powerful than any of us. My dad is a Gideon. He taught me the great faith of the Gideon organization: Put a Bible in a motel dresser drawer and it will work in wild and wonderful ways. The Bible does not need us. We need the Bible. Truth does not need us. We need the truth.

Academic Freedom

Professors should not try to suppress their peers. The courts should not try to close down the "open forum" of classrooms. Students, especially, should not become censors. As a student, don't try to stop professors from teaching what you think is wrong. Join in discussion, share ideas, take up your right to be a rational Christian on campus; however, do not think you have the right to trample on someone else's freedom.

Christians and non-Christians stand on the same freedom at secular universities. We cannot demand to be respected. We must earn respect. We must not whine about bad treatment. We must demand our rights in universities founded on liberality and the open-minded discussion of rational ideas.

That the Bible is divine revelation cannot be proven. It can only be known in our souls, much as many of us know in our souls that the Declaration of Independence is right when it declares that people are created equal with the right to life, liberty and the pursuit of happiness. As with any axiom, we know the authority of the Bible because of a self-evident commitment in our souls. Christians believe that such commitment is a gift of God. Most Christians believe that the Bible is divine revelation because of the corroborating testimony of the Holy Spirit within us. We know the authority of the Bible by a special grace of God. God apparently does not bestow that grace on everybody. Many of my honest friends in the university do not think the Bible is anything more than a human book. They feel no corroboration of its divinity. I cannot condemn them for not having a special gift of the Spirit. I cannot expect them to know what I feel in my soul. I can only expect them to trust me that I am as honest as they are in the pursuit of truth. Trusting my honesty, I can then expect them to judge my rationality just as academics judge the rationality of other faculty who uphold ideologies constructed on self-evident knowledge—such as civil rights, Marxism, democracy, free-enterprise capitalism, nihilism, classical liberalism and certain forms of feminism.

Divine Communication in the Classroom

Up until the late nineteenth century most academic disciplines had a place for knowledge revealed by God in the Bible—especially disciplines such as philosophy, mathematics, history, ethics, economics and psychology. Today those disciplines do not usually allow a student to use the Bible as a valid source of knowledge. But they could. If you want to use the Bible in these classes, you can ask your professors to allow you to write papers using alternative or older strategies of logic that broaden the normal, modern limits of academic disciplines.

In my history classes I will allow students to use the Bible. I require extra work to do it. The students must show that they understand that they are using an alternative knowledge source not normally used in history classes. They must show an understanding of the normal disciplinary methods of the profession and justify the use of the Bible as an alternative. I try to help students do this, but the students must be ambitious to do the work.

For example, one of my students wanted to write a paper proposing that God directed the course of American history up through the Civil War. He wanted to use evidence from the Bible that God sometimes directs national development, and he wanted to rely on the perceptions of early American leaders. I required him to show an understanding of the relationship of biblical evidence to standard forms of evidence. I advised him to point out the weaknesses and strengths of both types. He had to recognize that his type of study required that he emphasize introspection as a source of knowledge about the way the cosmos is run: his own introspection and the introspection of the many early American leaders who were sure that God was actively guiding them. Having established an understanding of his type of evidence and its relationship to more accepted professional practice among historians, he could then write a paper that was acceptable in a modern academic classroom.

Maybe you think I am weird to accept such a paper. I have asked my non-Christian colleagues, and they have told me they would accept such a paper. A few years ago a former student of mine wanted to study the apparitions of Mary the mother of Jesus in what was then Yugoslavia. He is a Roman Catholic and a firm believer that Mary is actively communicating with the modern world. He had already bought a plane ticket to Italy and was about to join a Roman Catholic Marian commune closely tied with the seers in Medjugorje. He wanted to get university credit for doing independent study on whether Mary was actually appearing. (Every student should do some independent research. Almost all universities have floating course titles that students can use to pursue their own interests. In an independent study course you can experiment with a professor on using the Bible for academic work.)

The student had taken my Medieval Civilization course. I knew his religious commitment, and I knew that he was smart and dedicated to the topic. The student and I developed a contract for work he would do in Italy, explaining that he was a firm believer who wanted to deal with the subject in an acceptable academic fashion. We submitted the contract to the academic vice chancellor, because the special kind of credit the student was going to receive required his signature. The vice chancellor signed and allowed me to take responsibility.

During six months of regular correspondence, we searched for an acceptable method for using the Bible and the accounts of seers in a university paper. During those months I sought the advice of other faculty. At a social gathering I asked several non-Christian faculty in philosophy, sociology and history what they thought the student would have to do to write an acceptable paper using the Bible and Marian seers. I hung microphones from the ceiling to record the conversation so I could send it to Italy. The consensus of these non-Christian professors was that it was academically respectable to accept a paper from a student demonstrating that Mary was actually appearing in Medjugorje if the student showed good understanding of the alternative character of the epistemology involved.

See! It is acceptable. Using the Bible and even Marian apparitions is acceptable to even non-Christian faculty. All good professors know that there are strengths and weaknesses to different ways of knowing and that what normally is taught in universities is not the only method of pursuing knowledge. You should want to be a rational Christian, and even non-Christian faculty can help you along the path. Remember, however, that Christianity is an outsider way of knowing in secular universities. The Christian must have enough ambition to do the extra work. The Christian must show an understanding of the normal, insider, procedures in order to then justify the use of alternative, outsider, procedures. The Christian must make a good argument for using the Bible or divine revelation in his or her papers. If the Christian doesn't do the extra work, then the professor will assume that the Christian just doesn't understand the normal rules of rational inquiry and academic communication.

Bible-based rationalism is not irrational. Your professor has not seriously studied epistemology and logic if he or she tells you that using the Bible or divine revelation is not a rational way of living. But be careful! We Christians cannot demand that Bible-based rationalism is the only right way to think. We must only demand our rightful place among the other forms of rationalism taught in universities. We have no reason to be embarrassed by our outsider methods; however, we have no reason to oppress others. Being rational has many roads. Pray for wisdom to know the right road. Pray for God's grace to support you intellectually. Pray for humility and love so that you can understand the motivations of the many who take different roads.

Analyzing the Bible

Professors, books and other students will sometimes tell you the Bible is full of contradictions as a flippant way to debunk the idea that the Bible has divine authority. If you hear a professor say such a thing in class, raise your hand and ask for an example of a contradiction. The vast majority of professors have never read the Bible. Most will not be able to give a precise example of a contradiction. There is no need to be antagonistic in such a situation. You are simply making an inquiry. All professors sometimes spout off about things they know little about. I have said things in the heat of class discussions that haunt me. A professor spouting off about the Bible or something Jesus said is not rare. A professor dismissing the Bible without ever having read it is also not rare. Raise your hand and give the professor an opportunity to clarify.

If your professor has read the Bible and gives some examples of contradictions, then you are in a situation where you and your professor can learn from each other. Grab the opportunity. That there are contradictions doesn't mean there isn't unity and truth. That there are contradictions doesn't mean that there are errors in the Bible. Most of what counts for contradiction can be resolved. Compare the accounts of who goes where when after Jesus is crucified. Compare the genealogies of Jesus in Matthew 1 and Luke 3. There are contradictions resolvable by rational speculation. If you have a will to resolve the contradictions, most are resolvable. The Bible calls us to bring our reason to it—not in the hope of finding errors but in the hope of learning.

The Bible is both simple and complicated. Since the early years of using sacred Scriptures, Christians have affirmed both populist and elitist views of Scripture. The populist view is democratic. It asserts that every listener, no matter how little educated, who comes to the Bible with openness will be spoken to by God. Jesus indicated that he may even speak especially to those without the advantages of education and those who occupy the margins of society. The greatest truths of Christianity—the divinity of Jesus, his love for us in birth, death and resurrection, and the importance of our responding to Jesus—are evident to any open-minded listener.

You and I have an elitist view. The elitist view does not have to deny the populist view; it can add to it. The fact that you are in college and reading this book categorizes you as one of the educated elite of the church who seek to know more about the religion that God has given us. You and I feel called by God to dig into the Bible for deeper truths and more knowledge. Because we dig into the Bible, we face its complications. The Bible rewards us as much as the populist thinkers, but elite thinkers often become confused, fall into debates and generally get caught in a morass on the frontiers between the infinite mind of God and the finite mind of humans.

Even the disciples were often confused by Jesus' teaching. At the Last Supper, recorded in Luke 22, Jesus tells the disciples that now is the time for them to take up swords. A few paragraphs later when Judas comes with the soldiers, one of the disciples starts to defend Jesus with a sword. Jesus rebukes him! The disciple was just trying to do what he was told. Jesus can be confusing.

In John 3 Jesus tells Nicodemus that he must be born again. (John 3 is one of the great chapters of the Bible and one of the best examples of how the Bible can be simple and complex at the same time.) Nicodemus, like us, tries to understand exactly what Jesus is saying, but Jesus is confusing sometimes.

We college-type Christians can easily get ourselves confused when we ask the Bible our sophisticated questions. This is not the Bible's problem. It is a problem caused by our limited minds coming into contact with the infinite mind of God.

Elite thinkers at secular universities have even more confusion with the Bible, since most of them have no interest in whether the Bible is really the Word of God. They are not like the disciples or Nicodemus, who desperately desired the truth from God. Most professors are quite content to analyze the Bible as if it were just another human document. Without the desire to find unities and divine communication, they emphasize disunities and look only for human voices.

We Can Murder When We Dissect

As in every other topic of study, university scholars have developed rational strategies of Bible study. Rational inquiry always requires a strategy, a method. Logical inquiry, as you may remember from chapter eight, is like geometry: breaking down things into bits of knowledge and then joining the bits to construct new knowledge. That new knowledge is rated probabilistically.

Academic Bible study requires a similar logical strategy: breaking the Bible into bits. Your ministers do it in their sermons. Jesus and Paul did it when they used the Hebrew Scriptures to explain something. The strategy is good, but we Christians must always be careful not to destroy the whole when we break the Bible down in order to more carefully analyze one thing. Remember Wordsworth's admonition: "We murder to dissect."

We can murder the living Word of God by dissecting it too much. We can also murder it by applying too many academic assumptions. I will take as an example a popular book used in universities and seminaries: Robert Alter's *The World of Biblical Literature.*

Alter is a reverent scholar of Jewish background who has helped many Christians and Jews to better understand the Bible. One of the things I like about his books is that he emphasizes unities in the Bible rather than disunities. He tries not to do too much dissection. His books on the literary qualities of the Bible are excellent. But Alter's books use the analytical method developed by literary scholars, which inevitably leads to diminishing the "holy" in Holy Scriptures. Altar discusses the holiness, but he wants to emphasize human analysis and leave religion to his readers.

Alter offers a scenario of a typical scholarly treatment of an Old Testament text:

> Two or more literary versions of the same set of events circulated in ancient Israel, let us say, in the early centuries of the Davidic monarchy. An editor chose to make one of these dominant but preserved bits and pieces of one or more competing versions and added his own editorial framework and occasional interventions.

Still later, probably early in the period of the return from Babylonian exile, a redactor gave final shape to the text, introducing local modifications of wording, adding some editorial framing and bridging, perhaps winnowing out certain materials, perhaps even incorporating bits of old traditions that had not hitherto been part of the text. All this suggests that the story of King David, even if he is one of the great characters of narrative literature, is built on a textual matrix utterly unlike that of any of the later major narratives in the West, where one master hand has shaped the tale from beginning to end.

The point of the scenario is that a story of King David in the Old Testament might have gone through many human hands and changed often before arriving in our modern Bibles.

Nowhere in the scenario is God mentioned. You the Christian must add God to the scenario. One option is to agree that all this happened and add that the Holy Spirit directed the process. An active God can still be communicating with us in the Bible even if the process of inspiration and authorship is split among many people and over a long period of time. Maybe God made the partially false versions of stories into one true story by working with a number of versions and story tellers. The "textual matrix" that Alter mentions means essentially that God might have inspired not one author in the way many of us think about writers, but many literary handlers.

But why can't there be just one author writing about David close to the time David lived? There can. Altar's scenario might be wrong, and Altar would admit it. What Altar is doing is creating the most probable scenario based on scholarly strategies. Let me digress from Alter's scenario to describe two principal types of scholarly strategies used by Bible scholars: a historical strategy and a commonsense strategy.

The Historical Strategy
The historical strategy makes generalizations about eras in history and expects people to speak and act within the context of their era. Scholars

look for anachronisms—things out of their time. Imagine a historian who discovers a Revolutionary War soldier's diary that reports that General Washington gave a speech in 1779 beginning: "We the soldiers of the United States of America, in order to form a more perfect army . . ." The historian will immediately be skeptical, because the phrase is much too similar to the opening sentence of the Constitution. The Constitution was written in 1787, *after* the war. The historian has three basic options: (1) the account is wholly false, along with probably the whole diary; (2) the person writing the account wrote of a true instance but later added some material that he believed Washington would have said; (3) the account is true. The last of these is the least probable because it requires such a stretch to explain the anachronism. (Here is a stretch: Washington, remembering his old war speech, could have suggested the opening phrase to those drafting the Constitution at a private meeting during the Constitutional Convention.) University scholars do not like to stretch for answers. Our rule: the less the stretch, the more probably true.

Bible scholars do the same. They look for anachronistic uses of phrases, words and concepts. They associate types of phrases, words and concepts with specific eras. A legal phrase found in the middle of an otherwise nonlegal narrative might be separated from the narrative and associated with an editor who lived in a time when there were a lot of legalisms used in the language. Bible scholars look for the most probable answer for the anachronism and avoid stretching to explain an anachronism.

But a historical strategy that works for reported speeches by George Washington does not necessarily work for accounts from the Bible. If God is inspiring biblical authors then it is quite possible that authors might, like prophets, see the future and use phrases, words and concepts out of their normal time. God and prophets in the Bible are by definition not bound by normal chronology and by any one era. When Moses uses ideas and phrases that seem more likely to fit in the language of the Jews a thousand years later, it doesn't have to mean that Moses did not say them. Inspiration is wilder than scholarly expectations.

The Commonsense Strategy

Allied with the historical strategy is the strategy of relying on "common sense." Biblical scholars often rely on commonsense probabilities of what seems like it should be. In 1 Samuel at two different times in King Saul's life the Bible tells us that the question is asked "Is Saul also among the prophets?" (1 Sam 10:11; 19:24). Many scholars using common sense consider it improbable that the same question would be asked at two different points during Saul's career. Since it is improbable, they then search for something more probable. Alter, in *The World of Biblical Literature,* quotes a Bible scholar who insists that the second use of the question must have been added later to the narrative by some editor.

But relying on common sense can be dangerous. Common sense says that the sun travels around the earth and that the earth is standing still in the universe. Common sense would have President Nixon destroy the Watergate tapes before anyone could hear them. Sometimes scholars using common sense make the Bible into their image rather than letting the Bible be itself.

Circular Thinking

The strategies of looking for anachronisms and relying on common sense which I have simplistically described often suffer from circular thinking. When I read an account of a speech by George Washington, I have thousands of independent sources to use for comparison and a very precise knowledge of the chronology of events. Bible scholars have far fewer sources to compare with and far less precise knowledge of chronology. They often rely on the Bible itself for the history that they then use to critique the Bible. This is circular thinking and is very weak scholarship.

For example, say a Bible scholar wants to figure out which of the letters attributed to Paul were actually written by Paul. First the scholar must figure out the phrasings, vocabulary and concepts that Paul used. The only place to find any writings by Paul is in the Bible. So the scholar reads all that is attributed to Paul in the Bible, then creates generalizations about Paul's style, vocabulary and patterns of thought. With these generalizations as the "true" Paul, the scholar then goes back and rereads the letters, deciding which fit them. If a letter does not fit, then the suggestion is made that it probably was not written by Paul in the first place.

The circularity is undeniable. When only one source exists, textual scholarship is unavoidably circular and, therefore, very weak. This weakness is characteristic of scholarly analysis of ancient texts and is known and accepted by universities. It is often the only or best strategy available, since so little is left from ancient times to do less circular comparisons.

Normalizing the Abnormal Bible

Both the historical and commonsense strategies are rooted in risky circular thinking. But deeper than the circular thinking are even riskier assumptions about the "normal." Both strategies emphasize the humanly normal. Both strategies work best for dealing with the normal course of time and normal people, events and writings. But what about the abnormal?

Let's go back to Alter's scenario where he mentions the "period of return from the Babylonian exile." This was an era of reorganization and legalism in the fifth and sixth centuries before Christ. Alter mentions redactors at work during the period—redactors are editors who reorganize and revise texts handed down from previous eras. As Alter indicates with his phrase "Still later, probably early in the period of the return from Babylonian exile," scholars use this time period as a catch-all for editorial work in the Old Testament, simply because it has the reputation as the period when someone would normally do such a thing. A lone redactor living quietly under Babylonian rule a hundred years earlier could have done the work; but such an abnormal individual working outside the norms of his era cannot be credited with the work, because the historical strategy of biblical scholars tends to deemphasize the possibility of abnormal situations. Bible scholars have to go for the most humanly probable, the normal, even though the less probable and abnormal might be the truth.

You see the problem. The Bible is an abnormal book about abnormal people and abnormal events. It is a book of prophets, miracles and God breaking into the normal course of events. An academic method rooted in generalizations about normality cannot deal effectively with such an abnormal book.

Another example: Daniel. The book of Daniel begins with the history of astonishing events, such as dream interpretation and being thrown into a lion's den, and ends with prophecies. In such a situation, most scholars feel obligated by their method to force the book into something more normal. They do this by making it fiction that might be loosely based on a real person written much later during a period after many of the supposed prophecies had already taken place. But for Christians, Daniel and his book have special corroboration: Jesus quotes "Daniel the prophet" in Matthew 24:15, implying that Daniel did write his book and was a prophet. But many biblical scholars override such corroboration by simply saying that Jesus was subject to the historical errors of his era. Thus the book of Daniel becomes normal fiction. Jesus becomes a normal person for his time. The Bible is made to make human sense by normalizing the abnormal.

Contradictions

Bible scholars, along with normalizing the abnormal, also rely on the simple logic that contradictory statements cannot both be true. But sometimes they can be true. If various places in the Old Testament books offer contradictory dates and numbers, then at least one of the dates or numbers must be false. This has to be—right? Not necessarily.

Did you know that George Washington was born on two different dates? He was born on February 11, 1731, and on February 22, 1732. As a historian, I know that both dates are true. There is no contradiction. By the English calendar his mother used, the first date is true. By the calendar that we use today, he was born on the second date. When Washington was a young man, the English Protestants finally admitted that the Roman Catholics on the Continent had a better calendar. In order to change calendars, the English government had to jump eleven days forward, and the date for calculating the new year was moved from March to January 1. Washington, born before the standardization of English and European calendars, has two birthdays.

We now live in an era of standardization. Western civilization follows standardized calendars, standardized weights and measures, standardized ways of calculating the reign of presidents and kings, and standardized methods for counting populations. Ancient times had no such standardizations. Any time we read an ancient text we should expect many contradictions of dates, measurements and numbers that are not really contradictions. The logic that contradictions indicate inaccuracies works sometimes for scholars but should not be treated as an inviolable law.

As a Christian listening to the variety of theories about the writing, dating and contradictory meanings in the Bible, you should be an active student. You must first bring God into the lecture, since your professor will avoid God. You then must keep in mind the weaknesses of scholarly strategies for handling the Bible. Overall, you must be wary about forcing the wild and spiritual into a box of the normal. Some of what you hear may be true, but don't throw off what you were taught by your church and family just because of one "Bible as Lit" course, or because a professor said the Bible was full of contradictions.

The Tendencies and Desires of Bible Scholarship
When I transferred as a junior to the University of California at Santa Barbara, I took many religious studies courses and had religious studies majors for roommates and friends. I had a crisis of faith about the Bible that lasted for several years. I never went so far as to think that the Bible was merely human literature, but every class I took and most of the religious discussions in my apartment tended to tear the Bible apart. An academic culture existed around me that *wanted* to find problems in the Bible. No student gets an A on a paper and no professor gets an article published in a respected journal for explaining how God spoke to them through the Bible. The incentives in scholar-

ship are toward impersonal and critical dissection. The incentives are also weighted toward the new. Professors need to find something new—a "hitherto unknown meaning of the phrase . . . ," a "hitherto unknown" redactor, or even a new interpretation of a central event in the Bible. A professor's career, pay raises and respect in the profession are largely tied to finding newness, while being a Christian consists largely living an old-style, traditional life, full of respect for the beliefs of the community of believers both past and present.

A good example of the tendencies toward dissection and newness in biblical scholarship is Jane Schaberg's study of Mary and the conception/birth narratives in the Bible, *The Illegitimacy of Jesus*. Schaberg is intellectually conscientious enough to explain her strategy for examining the birth narratives in the Bible. She writes that she is experimenting with a theory about an event to see if the theory could be reconciled with the earliest accounts of the event. Her primary interest is not what actually happened. She explains that she desires to make something useful out of the event for modern feminism. In order to do this she despiritualizes the conception of Jesus, interpreting early Christian and Jewish writings as indicating that Mary was raped.

Schaberg is not playing a false game with the Bible as a literary and historic text. By the standards of modern academic disciplines, the Bible is treated as a normal historical document. This means the Bible's account of an angel explaining to Mary what was happening cannot be accepted because it is spiritual rather than "natural." The natural, as academics suppose, is always more probable than the spiritual. Like any good historian, Schaberg accepts at face value the Bible's assertions that Mary was the mother of Jesus and that she gave birth in Bethlehem and subsequently returned to Nazareth, where she lived with her husband Joseph. Luke tells us these facts, and professional historians believe them because they seem normal and natural enough. But the spiritual stuff must be ignored. Schaberg's book was published by a good press and is academically respected because it offers the most plausible "natural" account of Mary's pregnancy—actually an almost unavoidable account if one arbitrarily rules out the angel's message.

By academic standards her book is a success. Schaberg dissects the story while looking for the most plausible explanation. She finds it and then interprets the new explanation in a way useful to a modern academic constituency. This is what gets rewarded in academic life. Being inspired by Mary doesn't normally get a student an A at a public university, nor does it get a Bible scholar published in mainline academic presses.

When I was a junior and senior at UCSB, I was uncomfortable with the academic emphasis on impersonal dissection and newness. I embraced the discipline of history as a way to love the past and its people. As much as I was uncomfortable with my religious studies courses and the academic tendencies of late-night Bible debates with my roommates, I was also driven by a desire not to be a gullible Christian. Gullibility is the result of irrationality and one of the worst academic sins. I continued to read the Bible regularly, but I found myself looking for contradictions, wary of being gullible. I began to keep a two-column pad of paper listing evidence for or against the Bible's authority. I prayed regularly for wisdom but felt like I was falling. Looking back, I think I was afraid of becoming like many of my professors, who were for the most part honorable and knowledge-able, but lacking an edge, lacking radical commitment, lacking lives that I wanted to emulate. On the other hand I no longer thought like my parents and began to think that I knew much more than the people I went to church with. Listening to a sermon, I was always able to find something wrong or naive.

A freeing moment came at a dinner with Ken Meredith, the Naza-rene minister from the church where I led a youth group. I told him—probably with an antagonistic desire to debate—that I disagreed with Nazarene theology. He said that was okay. I remember little of the conversation except that when talking about the problems in the Bible, he told me about the problem he most enjoyed: 1 Corinthians 1:13-17. Paul is exasperated with the Corinthians and thanks God that he did not baptize *any* of them—well, except for two guys—well, okay, there was a household of people—well, he's not sure how many he baptized, but that's not the point! Paul seems to have himself tied up in knots. Is Paul making an error? Is there a contradiction here? Is the Bible confused? My minister just laughed at the passage and reminded me—in effect—that the Bible is bigger than any of the boxes we try and put it in. A Christian can enjoy the problems in the Bible.

I confess that I have ever since taken great comfort in that passage and my minister's attitude of enjoying the Bible's problems and complexities while remaining reverent. I have since added another favorite passage: Titus 1:12-13. Paul, using a famous ancient conundrum, says that a Cretan is telling the truth when the Cretan says that all Cretans are liars. This is a double convolution of circular thinking. If all Cretans are liars then the Cretan saying this must be lying, and thus all Cretans are not liars so the Cretan saying this may not be lying. And so on. That's the first circle. Paul adds to it by saying the circle is true—but *what* is the truth? Paul must have been smiling when he dictated this.

The Bible is a collaboration between an infinite God and finite humans. Don't put it in a box. Live by it. Love it. Enjoy it.

What I learned from my Nazarene minister was a different approach. Instead of looking for problems, then making the problems into big problems, I learned the opposite tendency of looking for insights from God. The tendency of academic scholarship is distrust and skepticism; the tendency is to tear things apart, to normalize the abnormal and despiritualize the spiritual. Academic scholarship does hope to be positive, but only after first tending to be negative. Christianity is best understood when we tend toward the positive instead of the negative. We believe in order to understand rather than doubt in order to eventually understand.

Conclusion
Rules for the Direction of the Mind

René Descartes wrote a little logic book called *Rules for the Direction of the Mind.* I recommend it. It mostly describes the geometrical process of finding axioms and then constructing new knowledge out of those axioms. Descartes believed that God had revealed the axioms. And since God will not deceive us, we can use axioms as a firm foundation of knowledge. I want to give you a simple set of rules for rationality in the spirit of Descartes.

Rule 1. Look inside yourself. What do you know? You know many things about God, humanity and how you are to act. What you know inside yourself should give you confidence. Any good skeptic can play mind games with you to diminish your confidence, but your confidence can always be restored by the certainty of what you know inside. You know that you exist. You know that love and joy exist in an overwhelming way. You know that the creation exists around you and that it is wonderfully complex and beautiful. You know that a design and a designer exist, a source of love and joy. You have felt the hand of God in your life. You have met Jesus.

Rule 2. Rely on the communion of saints. If you are reading this book, I take it for granted that you also know the love of Jesus inside. I take it for granted that you have felt the grace of God in Jesus. Therefore you have adopted the teachings of the religion of Jesus. This puts you in a circle of knowledge, a community of Christians past, present and future. This communion of saints can give you confidence. The whole weight of deciding all questions does not lie on your shoulders. You can trust others within the community to share the load. Some you should trust because they have great authority because of their expertise, their wisdom and the fact that most of the community of Christians look to them for advice.

Rule 3. Rely on God's activity. You are not reaching out to a God far away. God is active in history and wants to help you in your pursuit of knowledge and wisdom. God is a hidden God in some ways. God is infinite and the human mind is only capable of grasping a finite glimmer of God's infinite light. God's thoughts and ways are not necessarily your thoughts and ways. However, you know that God is active. Jesus is God come down to earth. The Holy Spirit is God working in our souls and institutions throughout history. Pray for God's help in cultivating your rationality. Your rationality is part of the image of God in you. It is a pale image, but it is part of the image.

Rule 4. It takes patience to make the right decision. Never change any *important* part of your thinking until you pursue further information and seek wise advice. If something in a lecture or textbook makes you change from Democrat to Republican or from strong Christian beliefs to uncertain beliefs, you have changed too easily. You are being irrational to change fundamental beliefs merely on the basis of what you hear or read in classes. Fundamental beliefs should be changed only after long study in the library, consultation with many trusted and learned advisers, and sincere prayer for wisdom.

Classes, textbooks and even your whole undergraduate education must be understood as only a beginning. Your graduation is called "commencement" because it is a beginning. The discovery of knowledge, the pursuit of truth and the attainment of wisdom is a long pilgrimage. Never give up long-term goals and deep-seated understandings just because of some professors and classes.

Rule 5. God's activity is a grace. The knowledge you have inside you and the knowledge of the community of Christians is a grace. For some reason God has not yet chosen to be fully revealed in everyone's souls. Christians have a gift that sets them apart. We must be humble and loving. We must try to understand how best to invest this gift, while not condemning those who do not know in their souls what we know. We must be lights spreading the good news of the gospel and trying to awaken our colleagues to the grace of God. In secular universities we must work side by side with other people pursuing the truth. Don't hide what you know inside. Claim your rightful place next to non-Christians using the axioms that they know inside. However, do all in love. Too many Christians use the grace of having special knowledge in their soul as an excuse to suppress other people who don't have the same special knowledge. Never suppress people who pursue truth yet come up with some different truth from yours. As long as truth is being pursued, it is good. Expect an active God to be teaching us all as we search for truth.

Rule 6. Be open-minded. Christianity is dynamic. Knowledge is dynamic. Don't put your mind in a box. Don't put God in a box. New frontiers of knowledge are all around us. Share in the joy of pursuing truth, probing mysteries and discovering new knowledge. Universities are great centers for the dynamic use of the mind. Enjoy the university. Love the university.

Appendix
Reading, Suggested Reading & Notes

You should be a reading Christian. Not every Christian is responsible to be a reader, but you are. Education is a talent, a blessing. Don't bury it. Education is a responsibility, a duty. Don't shirk it. The multitude of illiterate Christians in poor countries and the multitude of poor Americans who have no leisure have their blessing: "Has not God chosen those who are poor in the eyes of the world to be rich in faith and to possess the kingdom he has promised to those who love him?" (Jas 2:5). By the fact that you are reading this I know you are from the educated elite of the world. You have education and leisure, two talents that put you at risk if you do not invest them well.

Don't waste your education by reading only magazines, self-help and fast-food books. Read and study your Bible. Read and study the great Christian writers of the past and present. Paul tells Christians who are of the educated elite that we must know how to defend our faith. For us the old monastic motto "Work is prayer" should also be understood as "Reading is prayer." The Holy Spirit speaks through books. The Holy Spirit can lead through books. Read to be in conversation with God and the conscientious thinkers of the past and present.

Do you lack the discipline, patience and self-control to be a reader? Don't worry about lacking such virtues. They are gifts of the Holy Spirit that God wants to give us. Ask, and the door shall be opened.

So, for a life of reading, where to start? Let me offer some rules and suggestions. Once you get started, you can leave my rules and suggestions far behind.

Rules for Reading

Rule 1. Read old books as well as new books—it is the way to avoid narrow-mindedness. Too many Christians think only in terms of ideas floating around today. Reading only new books is like drinking your own bath water. Old books are sometimes hard to read, but modern translations help.

Rule 2. Read biographies of the authors of the books you like. You can find short biographies in reference books. Never forget that books are born from the strengths and weaknesses of the people who write them.

Rule 3. Don't get bogged down in a book. Feel free to skip chapters or speed up to a part that interests you. If you find yourself wishing you were done with a book, then be done with it. Toss it aside and move on to another. When you find a good book, though, slow down to cherish it. Create your own index to the best passages on the back page. Read it more than once. Share it with a friend. Look for other books by the same author.

Rule 4. Your goal is to learn important and useful things, to be inspired, enlightened or challenged. Your goal is not to conquer a book. Your bookshelf is not a trophy case.

Books Behind This Book

Much in this handbook comes from *The Port-Royal Logic,* written primarily by Antoine Arnauld. *The Port-Royal Logic,* sometimes called *The Art of Thinking,* is a textbook for rational Christians written in France before 1662. For the next two hundred years it was very popular in schools and universities. When I first read it I was overwhelmed by its clarity, common sense, piety and rationality. I recommend it to you. There are many editions and translations available in your library or through interlibrary loan.

Here are the four other most important sources for the method of rationality I have presented:

1. John Locke, *An Essay Concerning Human Understanding* (1690). There are many shortened versions of this work. Avoid them. Editors cut out Locke's most Christian material. Get the whole version and go straight to book four— don't get bogged down in the first three parts of this massive book.

2. Nicholas Malebranche, *The Search After Truth,* trans. and ed. Thomas M. Lennon and Paul J. Olscamp (Columbus: Ohio State University Press, 1980). This is a big book, but if nothing else, just spend a rainy afternoon wandering in it.

3. I learned much from a number of ancient, medieval and Renaissance logicians noted and discussed in *Aristotelian and Cartesian Logic at Harvard: Morton's "System of Logick" and Brattle's "Compendium of Logick,"* ed. Rick Kennedy (Boston: Colonial Society of Massachusetts, 1995).

4. Do these books sound boring? Rationality is a wild and wonderful endeavor that requires much heart. No book has taught me more about this than Blaise Pascal's *Pensées*—a book of thoughts wrestling with the mind's frailty.

For general reading on university life and values, wander the college histories section of your library. Read the chapters about "student life" and the academic disciplines in which you are most interested. Go to your university bookstore and buy the history of your campus. Biographies usually have a chapter on the life of their subject at college. *The Oxford Book of Oxford,* ed. Jan Morris (Oxford: Oxford University Press, 1978), is full of interesting incidents in college life from the Middle Ages to today and makes one realize that some things never change. *God and Man at Yale: The Superstitions of Academic Freedom* (Chicago: Regnery, 1951) is an angry book by William F. Buckley Jr. when he had just graduated. Ari L. Goldman is less angry when he talks about his classes, teachers and friends in *The Search for God at Harvard* (New York: Ballantine, 1991). Much of Thomas Merton's *The Seven Storey Mountain* (New York: Harcourt Brace, 1948) is about his spiritual search while in college. Merton biographies often give a fascinating picture of Cambridge University and Columbia University and focus on Merton's close relationship with one professor, Mark Van Doren. Keith and Gladys Hunt's *For Christ and the University: The Story of InterVarsity Christian Fellowship of the U.S.A.* (Downers Grove, Ill.: Inter-Varsity Press, 1991) has lots of stories of students accomplishing great things. Paul V. Turner's *Campus: An American Planning Tradition* (New York: Architectural History Foundation/Cambridge, Mass.: MIT Press, 1984) will help you understand the ideas behind your surroundings.

The academic novel is a full-blown literary genre that tends to exaggerate and is often very sarcastic but reveals many of the essential joys and foibles of university life. There are thousands of these novels. Kingsley Amis's *Lucky*

Jim (New York: Penguin, 1961) is a classic, but David Lodge's *Small World: An Academic Romance* (London: Secker & Warburg, 1984) is a personal favorite. John Kenneth Galbraith's *A Tenured Professor* (Boston: Houghton Mifflin, 1990) gives an insider's look at the life of a Harvard economist. A pleasant view of student life at UC Berkeley is presented in Clarkson Crane's *On the Western Shore* (Salt Lake City: Peregrine Smith, 1985). I'll slip in a movie: *Educating Rita.*

As for university histories, Robert S. Shepard's *God's People in the Ivory Tower: Religion in the Early American University* (Brooklyn, N.Y.: Carlson, 1991) deals with the end of the nineteenth century. Bruce Kucklick's *Churchmen to Philosophers: From Jonathan Edwards to John Dewey* (New Haven, Conn.: Yale University Press, 1985) and *The Rise of American Philosophy* (New Haven, Conn.: Yale University Press, 1977) give an overview of nineteenth-century and early-twentieth-century developments in philosophy departments. The best general histories of modern universities are Laurence Vesey's *The Emergence of the American University* (Chicago: University of Chicago, 1965) and George Marsden's *The Soul of the American University: From Protestant Establishment to Established Non-belief* (New York: Oxford University Press, 1994). For the largest context, see Lawrence A. Cremin's three-volume history, *American Education* (New York: Harper & Row, 1970-1988). Steven C. Rockefeller's *John Dewey: Religious Faith and Democratic Humanism* (New York: Columbia University Press, 1991) studies one of the most crucial education figures of the twentieth century; Harry S. Ashmore's *Unseasonable Truths: The Life of Robert Maynard Hutchins* (Boston: Little, Brown, 1989) looks at another.

Today there is a wave of books attacking universities and professors. Of the ones I've read, most are very narrow-minded but are based in truth. I recommend Page Smith's *Killing the Spirit: Higher Education in America* (New York: Penguin, 1990). More positive is Lesslie Newbigin's *Foolishness to the Greeks: The Gospel and Western Culture* (Grand Rapids, Mich.: Eerdmans, 1986), which is not specifically about universities but makes an excellent case that Christians must be engaged in the secular world of Western rationality. Mark Noll's *The Scandal of the Evangelical Mind* (Grand Rapids, Mich.: Eerdmans, 1994) also makes a strong case more specifically related to evangelicals and university disciplines. James W. Sire's *Chris Chrisman Goes to College* (Downers Grove, Ill.: InterVarsity Press, 1993) is also good.

On the academic use of authorities, see C. A. J. Coady's *Testimony: A*

Philosophical Study (Oxford: Clarendon, 1992). It is deep academic philosophy but rewards any reader who will go through it carefully. Trust and the role of testimony is a matter little talked about in universities but is crucial. My position on the generally inconsistent use of testimony by historians is more fully developed in "Miracles in the Dock: A Critique of the Historical Profession's Special Treatment of Alleged Spiritual Events," *Fides et Historia* 26 (1995).

I don't know where to start you on the Bible—most of the literature is so controversial. Start with your minister, who is probably highly trained in various perspectives on the Bible and will have books to lend you. Next, go to the library and ask for the various Bible dictionaries and encyclopedias. Browse. Look for subjects that interest you: a biographical sketch of a disciple, archaeological information about places or a history of how the books of the Bible were collected. Make sure you wander in more than one source and pick from different publishers. Try to get a broad range of information and interpretations. Look at the bibliography at the ends of the short articles, and seek out further information. The three-volume *Cambridge History of the Bible* (Cambridge: Cambridge University Press, 1975) is very informative. Mark Noll's *Between Faith and Criticism: Evangelicals, Scholarship and the Bible in America* (New York: Harper & Row, 1986) is also very good.

The positive approach I take in this book is largely based on the influence of several of my professors at UC Santa Barbara. Jeffrey B. Russell especially modeled for me the integration of Christianity in the secular classroom. He is now retired from the undergraduate classroom, but you can still see some of the vigor of his thought in his four volumes on the devil. Jeff firmly asserts his belief in a personal devil who is actively encouraging evil in our world in the first chapter of each of these volumes, published by Cornell University Press: *The Devil: Perceptions of Evil from Antiquity to Primitive Christianity* (1977), *Satan: The Early Christian Tradition* (1981), *Lucifer: The Devil in the Middle Ages* (1984) and *Mephistopheles: The Devil in the Modern World* (1986). I know of no historian working today who better models rational inquiry into spiritual subjects.

On Christian colleges I recommend Christopher Derrick's *Escape from Skepticism: Liberal Education As If Truth Mattered* (Peru, Ill.: Sherwood, Sugden, 1977), which is rooted in the ideas of St. Thomas Aquinas and praises life at a small Roman Catholic college. *New Catholic World* magazine had a special issue called *Catholic Higher Education in America: Challenges for a Third Century* in September/October 1988. From the Protestant perspective I recommend *Making Higher Education Christian: The History and Mission of Evangelical Colleges in America,* ed. Joel A. Carpenter and Kenneth W. Shipps (Grand Rapids, Mich.: Christian University Press, 1987).

Notes to Quotes

Preface

Charles Malik, *The Two Tasks* (Winchester, Ill.: Cornerstore, 1980), pp. 29-34, quoted in Mark A. Noll, *The Scandal of the Evangelical Mind* (Grand Rapids, Mich.: Eerdmans, 1994), p. 25.

Bonaventure, *The Mind's Journey into God,* trans. Ewart Cousins, in *The Classics of Western Spirituality,* ed. Richard Payne (New York: Paulist, 1978), pp. 55-57.

Chapter 1: The Village

Henry Rosovsky, *The University: An Owner's Manual* (New York: W. W. Norton, 1990).

Chapter 2: The Knowledge Industry

Thomas D. Clark, *Indiana University* (Bloomington: Indiana University Press, 1970), 2:49.

Chapter 3: Faculty & Fellowship

Scott Heller, "Art Historian as Provocateur," *The Chronicle of Higher Education,* August 17, 1994, p. A9.

Henry Peacham, "Of the Time of Learning, Duty of Masters and What the Fittest Method to be Observed," in *The Compleat Gentleman* (1622).

Alexander Campbell Fraser, *Biographia Philosophica: A Retrospect* (Edinburgh: William Blackwood and Sons, 1905), pp. 53-58.

John Veitch, "A Memoir of Dugald Stewart," in Dugald Stewart, *Biographical Memoirs* (Edinburgh: n.p., 1858), pp. xxvii-xxviii.

Chapter 4: Pursuing Truth

"Will the Circle Be Unbroken," author unknown.

C. A. J. Coady, *Testimony: A Philosophical Study* (Oxford: Clarendon, 1992).

G. K. Chesterton, *Orthodoxy* (Garden City, N.Y.: Doubleday/Image, 1959), pp. 47-48.

James D. Watson, *The Double Helix: A Personal Account of the Discovery of the Structure of DNA,* ed. Gunther S. Trent (New York: W. W. Norton, 1980).

G. H. Hardy, *A Mathematician's Apology* (Cambridge: Cambridge University Press, 1940), chap. 7.

John Locke, *Essay Concerning Human Understanding,* bk. 4, chap. 19, sect. 1.

Chapter 5: University Values

Indiana University Southeast's mission statement is quoted from the *IUS Faculty Manual,* 1987, p. 1.

Thomas Jefferson, "A Bill for Establishing Religious Freedom," in his *Writings,* ed. Merrill D. Peterson (New York: Library of America, 1984), pp. 346-47.

Origen, *On First Principles,* trans. G. W. Butterworth (Gloucester, Mass.: Peter Smith, 1973), p. xxvii.

Loren W. Partridge, *John Galen Howard and the Berkeley Campus: Beaux-Arts Architecture in the "Athens of the West"* (Berkeley: Berkeley Architectural Heritage Association, 1978), p. 31.

Chapter 6: Disunities at the Modern University

Judith R. Goodstein, *Millikan's School: A History of the California Institute of Technology* (New York: W. W. Norton, 1991), p. 194.

Chapter 7: The Progress of Knowledge

Francis Bacon, *New Organon,* bk. 1, chap. 84. In the interest of not misleading, Bacon's famous line is "For rightly is truth called the daughter of time, not of authority." Bacon was wrong about authority. He tended to polemic extremes in his rhetoric.

Chapter 8: Being Aware of Limits & Strategies

Aristotle *Analytica Posteriora* 100b, trans. G. R. G. Mure, in *The Works of Aristotle,* ed. W. D. Ross (Oxford: Clarendon, 1928).

Charles Darwin, *The Descent of Man,* quoted in Duane P. Schultz and Sydney Ellen Schultz, *A History of Modern Psychology,* 4th ed. (San Diego, Calif.: Harcourt Brace Jovanovich, 1987), p. 123.

Steven Pinker, review of *The Language Instinct* by Michael D. Coe, *The New York Times Book Review,* February 27, 1994, p. 7.

Ed Regis, *Who Got Einstein's Office? Eccentricity and Genius at the Institute for Advanced Study* (New York: Addison-Wesley, 1987), p. 211.

For Kelvin's dictum, see Robert K. Merton, David L. Sills and Stephen M. Stegler, "The Kelvin Dictum and Social Science: An Excursion into the History of an Idea," *Journal of the History of the Behavioral Sciences* 20 (1984): 319-31.

Newton and Leibniz's interchanges on this subject were conducted through an intermediary. See *The Leibniz-Clarke Correspondence,* ed. H. G. Alexander (Manchester, U.K.: Manchester University Press, 1956). For Newton's speculation that the omnipresent God is the cause of gravity at every moment, see the discussion and footnotes in Richard Westfall, *Never at Rest: A Biography of Isaac Newton* (Cambridge: Cambridge University Press, 1980), pp. 647-48.

Chapter 9: The Mind-Boggling Life of Being Rational

Blaise Pascal, *Pensées,* trans. A. J. Krailsheimer (London: Penguin, 1966), p. 85. (The numbering of the many editions of the *Pensées* varies. This phrase will usually be in either number 182 or number 272.)

Thomas V. Morris, *Making Sense of It All: Pascal and the Meaning of Life* (Grand Rapids, Mich.: Eerdmans, 1992); also *God and the Philosophers: The Reconciliation of Faith and Reason,* ed. Thomas V. Morris (New York: Oxford University Press, 1994); and Clyde Crews, *Fundamental Things Apply: Reflecting on Christian Basics* (Notre Dame, Ind.: Ave Maria, 1983).

Charlotte Elliott, "Just As I Am."

Chapter 10: Decisions

Einstein is quoted in Ronald W. Clark, *Einstein: The Life and Times* (New York: World, 1971), pp. 340, 345-46.

John Henry Newman, *Apologia Pro Vita Sua* (Garden City, N.Y.: Image, 1956), pp. 140-41, 264. Read also page 139: "It is faith and love which give to probability a force which it has not in itself." As for the quote on doubt, I can't find it but I am sure he said it. I confess also that I am unable to find "Be comforted, small one, in your smallness." I know it is somewhere in the Narnia series by C. S. Lewis.

Carl G. Jung, *Memories, Dreams, Reflections,* recorded and ed. Aniela Jaffé, trans. Richard and Clara Winston (New York: Vintage, 1965).

Stephen J. Gould, "Impeaching a Self-Appointed Judge," *Scientific American,* July 1992, p. 119.

Phillip E. Johnson, *Darwin on Trial* (Downers Grove, Ill.: InterVarsity Press, 1991).

Phillip E. Johnson, "The Religion of the Blind Watchmaker," *Perspectives on Science & Religion*, March 1993, p. 46. Johnson quotes from Stephen Jay Gould, "In Praise of Charles Darwin," *Discover*, February 1982.

Quintilian *Institutio Oratoria* 1. 6; and Augustine *On the Profit of Believing* 26.

Chapter 11: The Bible in Class

Wendell Berry, "The Loss of the University," *Home Economics* (New York: North Point, 1987), p. 92.

Mindy Weinreb, "A Question a Day: A Written Conversation with Wendell Berry," in *Wendell Berry*, ed. Paul Merchant (Lewiston, Idaho: Confluence, 1991), p. 30.

Robert Alter, *The World of Biblical Literature* (New York: Basic Books, 1992), pp. 3-4.

Jane Schaberg, *The Illegitimacy of Jesus: A Feminist Theological Interpretation of the Infancy Narratives* (San Francisco: Harper & Row, 1987).